Courtship, Valentine's Day, 1918

Courtship, Valentine's Day, 1918

HORTON FOOTE

*Three Plays
from The
Orphans' Home Cycle*

Introduction by
REYNOLDS PRICE

GROVE PRESS
New York

Published simultaneously in Canada
Printed in the United States of America

LIBRARY OF CONGRESS CATALOGING-IN-PUBLICATION DATA
Foote, Horton.
Courtship ; Valentine's Day ; 1918 : three plays
from "The orphans' home cycle."

I. Title: Courtship. II. Title: Valentine's Day.
III. Title: 1918.
PS3511.0344C69 1987   812'.54   86-31970

ISBN 978-0-8021-5155-1

Grove Press
an imprint of Grove/Atlantic, Inc.
841 Broadway
New York, NY 10003

Distributed by Publishers Group West

www.groveatlantic.com

13 14 15 16   10 9 8 7 6 5 4 3

To the memory of my parents, Albert Horton and Hallie Brooks Foote, and to my wife, Lillian Vallish Foote.

Contents

New Treasure

SIMPLICITY OF MEANS and lucidity of results may not be the universal aims of art throughout the world, but they're very nearly so. The brute suavity of French cave-paintings, the mathematically sophisticated but visually spare shapes of Greek temples, the calligraphic and encoded elegance of Oriental scroll-painting, the Bach Prelude in C, a William Blake lyric, the final movement of Beethoven's last piano sonata (opus 111), an Appalachian ballad—who doesn't love them all? Millions may resist the polyphonic magnificence, wit, and ecstasy of Bernini's Saint Teresa; but who has not surrendered to Michelangelo's youthful Virgin of the *Pietà?*

Yet how to describe, or discuss, any such masterpiece? How—in Chesterton's joke—to play the Venus de Milo on a trombone? It's a famous and lamentable limitation of modern aesthetic criticism—whether of the graphic and plastic arts, literature, music, or performance—that it has proved generally helpless in the presence of apparent "simplicity," the illusory purity of means and ends toward universally comprehensible results. Where is there a genuinely illuminating discussion of Blake's "Tyger," Gluck's "Dance of the Blessed Spirits," or Joan Baez's traversals of the Child ballads?—one that helps us understand *how* and, above all, *why* such complex but supremely satisfactory ends are achieved in such small and evidently transparent vehicles. As readers' minds are most engaged, in narrative fiction, by wicked or at least devious characters, so the mechanistic methods of modern critics require complexity of means before their intricate gears can begin to grind.

Thus (since I'm here to celebrate three plays) Shakespeare is the critic's darling among dramatists. Apart from questions of relative depth and durability of interest, he provides the critic an apparently infinite parade of artifice —one which anyhow shows no sign of exhausting in their multitudinous hands.

In Europe at least, other dramatists—Racine, Ibsen, Strindberg, Chekhov, and Shaw—have elicited memorable and still useful studies. But what American dramatist has yet received similar treatment? Admittedly, our first great playwright has been dead fewer than forty years. But again, Eugene O'Neill worked with sufficient awkwardness of means toward his broad and deep effects to make him unattractive to a tribe of critics energized primarily by technical adroitness. An almost identical assertion might be made for our second internationally significant dramatist, Tennessee Williams. The straightforward urgency and eloquence of his best early work— the lean balladic lament of *Glass Menagerie* or the arpeggiated rising howl of *Streetcar*—have yet to receive sustained helpful attention from critics.

Any sympathetic viewer of the recent films and plays of Horton Foote is likely to share the critics' dilemma. Were you as deeply moved as I was by his *Tender Mercies*

(1983)? Then can you tell me why? Explain to me how actors—even as perfect as those he found, even so resourceful a director—could employ so few and such rhetorically uncomplicated speeches toward the flawless achievement of such a calmly profound and memorable face-to-face contemplation of human degradation and regeneration. I confidently suggest that even St. Augustine in his *Confessions* went no farther toward the heart of that luminous dark mystery than Horton Foote. And I—a novelist, poet, playwright, and critic—cannot hope to begin to tell you how he has made that longest and hardest of journeys. I can only urge you to look and then agree or disagree.

In the case of *The Orphans' Home*, his monumental cycle of nine related plays, I'm in better luck—though only to this extent. The plays are now being published by Grove Press, and the volume I introduce here is the first of a proposed three. Though two of the plays have been filmed and several others performed on stage, no one has yet seen all of them in coherent productions, and given the scattered disorganization of the American commercial theatre and the poverty of the lively regional companies, no one is likely to see all nine any year soon. But soon all will be readable, and the black-and-white outlines of Foote's large scheme will be at least discernible.

For what these texts—and his recent films—demonstrate is how unquestionably Foote is the supreme musician among our great American playwrights. More even than with Tennessee Williams, Foote's method (and his dilemma) is that of the composer. His words are black notes on a white page—all but abstract signals to the minds of actor and audience, signs from which all participants in the effort (again all those at work on both sides of the stage or camera, including the audience) must make their own musical entity.

Take the case of *1918*, the third play here. A careful

reading of its printed text will provide the pleasures we expect of well-made and intensely felt drama—the gracefully attenuated line of suspense, the nearly devastating crisis, the unexpected but credible and warm resolution. Despite the scarcity of stage descriptions or directions to the actors, we can (if we're ideally cooperative) construct our own series of pictures of small-town early twentieth-century Texas, not that different from small-town America anywhere else—or small-town bourgeois France of the same time, for that matter. But nowhere can we point to speeches of an extraordinary or heightened eloquence, language of an "unreal" intensity or rhythm. Memory is allowed to flow and blossom (for all the plays are loosely based on the history of Foote's own families) into universal emotion but only within the strict verbal channels of the quotidian, the daily norm. Language is pruned and shaped but not visibly transformed.

See the film of *1918* though. And there, within the physical confines of a modest budget, a small company of beautifully restrained and emotionally transparent players perform the minimal text with such grave musical skill as to achieve a final effect of genuinely transcendent volume. From the bare lines of Horton Foote's original text —and from nowhere else really, except the voluble faces of the actors—there pours finally a joyful and unanswerably powerful psalm of praise: Suffering (to the point of devastation) is the central human condition and our most unavoidable mystery. Yet we can survive it and sing in its face. The only tonal parallels that come easily to mind— for similar findings, wisdom, and credibility—are the conclusion of *A Long Day's Journey into Night* or the rapturous final claim of Chekhov's *Uncle Vanya*. Yet even they, for all their grandeur of human love and pardon, are not bolstered by such a glacial weight of evidence as Foote provides in the prior and succeeding plays of his cycle, rich as it is in all the emotions from farce to tragedy to transcendence.

Courtship and *Valentine's Day* are parallel achievements—indeed, the three are grouped as numbers five, six, and seven in the cycle of nine. When all three volumes of the series have appeared, and *The Orphans' Home* can then be seen whole and entire, I'm confident it will take its rightful earned place near the center of our largest American dramatic achievements—a slowly generated, slowly won, apparently effortless, surprisingly wide vision of human life that flowers before our patient incredulous eyes with an opulent richness of fully communicated pleasure, comprehension, and usable knowledge: a permanent gift.

—Reynolds Price
October 1986

Courtship

Characters

ELIZABETH VAUGHN
LAURA VAUGHN
MR. VAUGHN
MRS. VAUGHN
LUCY
SARAH
HORACE ROBEDAUX
STEVE TYLER

Place: The Vaughn House, Harrison, Texas
Time: 1915

At rise we see part of the large gallery surrounding the VAUGHN *house. On the gallery are two wicker rocking chairs, a wicker table and another wicker table against the wall of the house. We can see that portion of the house that is the music room, also used as a sitting room, defined by a scrim and lit from time to time.*

During the play, couples dance in and out . . . not seen by the other characters present on the stage. The dances are of the period: waltzes, fox trots, turkey trot, cake walk, etc.

ELIZABETH VAUGHN *enters. She stands on the gallery of the house, listening to dance music in the distance.* LAURA, *her sister, enters with tray.*

LAURA: Oh, it's nice to be home again.

ELIZABETH: You enjoy school, don't you?

LAURA: Yes, but it's nice to be home with your family. When you were off at school, didn't you always like coming home for vacation?

ELIZABETH: Yes, I did.

LAURA: Next year Papa says he wants me to go to school in Virginia. I guess I'll go if he wants me to, but it is awfully far away.

ELIZABETH: I know all your friends are glad to have you home.

LAURA: I think so. So much has gone on since I've been away I don't think I'll ever catch up with all the news. (*Pause. She puts her arm around* ELIZABETH.) I'm glad we're having this chance to talk by ourselves. I missed you.

ELIZABETH: And I missed you.

LAURA: Are you enjoying teaching piano?

ELIZABETH: Yes, I am.

LAURA: All those years of practice paid off.

ELIZABETH: I suppose.

LAURA: I don't know what I'll do when I graduate. Mama says I should start a kindergarten class. I could teach in the sun room. (*Pause.*) You can hear the orchestra so plain tonight.

ELIZABETH: Yes.

LAURA: I think it is a shame Papa has never allowed us to go to dances. Annie Gayle says her mother thinks he acts so strict because of how Uncle Billy ended. Do you remember Uncle Billy's first wife?

ELIZABETH: Kind of.

LAURA: I barely do. I remember the second one though.

ELIZABETH: I guess we all remember Aunt Asa.

(MRS. VAUGHN *comes out on the porch.*)

MRS. VAUGHN: Come in later, girls, and get a visit with your aunts. It would please your father.

ELIZABETH: Yes Ma'am.

LAURA: How long are they going to stay this time?

MRS. VAUGHN: They will be here through September just like they are every year, waiting out the storm season.

Maybe tonight you could play some pieces on the piano for them. (*She goes back in.*)

LAURA: Did you see the dress Priscilla wore to the dance tonight?

ELIZABETH: Yes, a low-cut princess style.

LAURA: You know what I heard this afternoon? That Priscilla's mother and father had to get married. Have you ever heard that?

ELIZABETH: Yes.

LAURA: And I heard that Priscilla knows that she is illegitimate and that's why she says she will never marry, because she's so mortified about being illegitimate. Had you ever heard that?

(*A couple dances in and out.*)

ELIZABETH: Yes. (*Pause.*) Alice's mother made her the most beautiful dress I think I've really ever seen. Pale green chiffon. She tried it on for me this afternoon. She looked so pretty in it. (*She whispers.*) I got invited to the dance.

LAURA: Who asked you?

ELIZABETH: I got asked twice. Steve Farley and Horace Robedaux.

(*A couple dances in and out. A clock strikes nine.*)

LAURA: I think Horace Robedaux is very good looking. So do a lot of other girls here, too. I hear he's very wild.

ELIZABETH: I don't think he's all that wild. If I tell you a secret, promise you won't tell anyone?

LAURA: I won't.

ELIZABETH: I like him a lot. He asked me to go to the picture show with him tomorrow night.

LAURA: Are you going?

ELIZABETH: Yes I am.

(*A couple dances in and out.*)

I wish we were at the dance. (*She looks around carefully, then whispering . . .*) I've learned to dance.

LAURA: Have you?

ELIZABETH (*sings a snatch of "Red Wing"*): Do you like that song?

LAURA: Yes, I do. And I like that song the orchestra is playing. (*Pause.*) Elizabeth, you're so much quieter than you used to be.

ELIZABETH: Am I? (*She puts her arm around* LAURA.) I don't mean to be.

LAURA: Elizabeth.

ELIZABETH: Yes?

(*A couple dances in and out.*)

LAURA: I heard Syd Joplin was killed last week in El Campo.

ELIZABETH: Yes, I heard that too.

LAURA: Did it make you sad when you heard it?

ELIZABETH: Yes.

LAURA: Annie Gayle said you were in love with him and that you told Harriet Grey you were going to run off and marry him since Mama and Papa wouldn't let you see him. Did you say that?

ELIZABETH: I guess I did. (*Pause.*) I was in love with him. At least I thought I was. I used to go to the picture show every time the doors opened just to get a look at him.

LAURA: Are you still in love with him?

ELIZABETH: No.

LAURA: Were you ever really in love with him?

ELIZABETH: I thought so.

LAURA: Annie Gayle said he asked you to marry him.

ELIZABETH: He did.

LAURA: Do you think if you had married him you would have still loved him?

ELIZABETH: No.

LAURA: Wouldn't it be terrible to think you were in love with someone, marry them and then find out you weren't?

ELIZABETH: Yes.

LAURA: Annie Gayle said you are only attracted to wild boys.

ELIZABETH: Why did she say that?

LAURA: That's what her mother told her. Are you?

ELIZABETH: I don't think so.

LAURA: Horace Robedaux is wild and you're attracted to him.

ELIZABETH: I told you, I don't think he's so wild. I certainly don't think he's as wild as they all make out.

LAURA: I would be afraid of marrying a wild boy. They don't ever stay home and they drink and gamble and get into debt and neglect you and you die of a broken heart. Anyway, that's what Mama says.

ELIZABETH: But if you don't marry someone you love
. . . What then?

LAURA: Mama says if he's rich it usually works out all
right. Just think if you married Syd Joplin you would have
been a widow by now, wearing black.

(LUCY *and* SARAH, *Mr. Vaughn's sisters, come out on the gallery.*)

LUCY: Are your sweet mama and papa out here?

ELIZABETH: No Ma'am. I don't know where they are.

SARAH: I thought I heard them talking out here.

ELIZABETH: No Ma'am.

LUCY: Are you enjoying being home, Laura?

LAURA: Yes Ma'am.

(LUCY *and* SARAH *exit.*)

LAURA: Aunt Lucy was a widow at thirty-two, wearing
black, with four children to take care of. I guess if you are
a widow at thirty-two with four children to take care of
you couldn't get anybody to marry you.

ELIZABETH: Her husband, Captain Stewart, was twenty
years older than she was. He was a Captain in the Confed-
erate Army.

LAURA: Did you ever see him?

ELIZABETH: No. He was dead before I was born. As a girl
Aunt Lucy was in love with Cousin Irvin Murray, but
Grandma wouldn't let them marry because they were first
cousins, but neither of them ever loved anyone else and
every day at four o'clock Cousin Irvin would pass Aunt
Lucy's house on his way home and rain or shine she

would be sitting on the gallery waiting for him to pass by and they would bow to each other.

LAURA: I wonder if they still love each other.

ELIZABETH: I don't know. When Captain Stewart died, Aunt Lucy and her children moved in with Grandma Vaughn, and Cousin Irvin and his family moved to Houston. (*Pause.*) Sybil Thomas got into trouble.

LAURA: No.

ELIZABETH: I hear she is four months pregnant.

LAURA: Oh, my God! Who by?

ELIZABETH: Leo Theil.

LAURA: Poor Sybil Thomas! I wonder if anybody in our family had that happen to them. I'd be so mortified. I'd jump in the river and drown. Wouldn't you?

ELIZABETH: I don't know. I wouldn't want it to happen, but I don't think I'd jump in the river.

LAURA: What would you do?

ELIZABETH: I don't know.

LAURA: Who do you think the wildest girl in town is?

ELIZABETH: Bertie Harris.

LAURA: Do you think all the Harris girls are fast?

ELIZABETH: More or less. Bertie is. Jocey Bell is. Their grandmother, Mrs. Lawson, is a dope fiend.

LAURA: How do you know?

ELIZABETH: I heard Mama tell Mrs. Cookenboo she takes paregoric.

LAURA: Oh, go on.

ELIZABETH: She does too.

LAURA: Don't tell me any more bad things. Tell me something nice.

ELIZABETH: Like what?

LAURA: I don't care. Just something nice. I don't want to talk any more about unhappy marriages and wild sisters and dope fiends. (*Pause.*) What about Aunt Asa?

ELIZABETH: I thought you didn't want to talk any more about wild women?

LAURA: Just tell me about her and we'll change the subject.

ELIZABETH: To tell you the truth I don't remember too much about her. I remember she got herself up like a carnival queen at Mardis Gras time and I remember . . . She was drunk when Uncle Billy was dying. I went in with Papa and Mama to see him just before he died and I knew she was drunk because of the loud way she was talking and carrying on. She kept saying over and over "There's nothing wrong with Billy; he'll be up in a day or two, good as new." (*Pause.*) I heard Mama and Mrs. Cookenboo talking once and they said she had behaved scandalously.

LAURA: How?

ELIZABETH: Well . . . I'm not sure. I don't think she was faithful to Uncle Billy for one thing.

LAURA: She wasn't?

ELIZABETH: I don't think so. And you know Miss Dorothy Stonehill? She had a young sister, and Aunt Asa had her over at the house a lot and there was a lot of talk I never understood about . . . Iris, that was Miss Dorothy's sister's name, and (SARAH *enters music room*) how Aunt Asa introduced her to the wrong kind of men and goodness, I don't know what all . . . (*Pause.*) Laura, when I slept over at Rita's night before last, we slipped out after her mother and father went to bed. And Horace Robedaux and Addis Miller came by in a buggy and we went riding with them.

(MR. VAUGHN *enters music room.* MRS. VAUGHN *comes to the front door.*)

MRS. VAUGHN: Come in girls, we want you to play for us now.

(LAURA *goes to her mother and they go into the house.* ELIZABETH *stands for a moment listening to the music and then she goes inside.* MRS. VAUGHN *and* LAURA *enter the music room.* MR. VAUGHN *and the* AUNTS *are seated near the piano.* MRS. VAUGHN *and* LAURA *come in.* ELIZABETH *enters.*)

MRS. VAUGHN: Sis Lucy has made a request.

SARAH: It wasn't Sis Lucy. It was me.

MRS. VAUGHN: I'm sorry. It was Sis Sarah. She wants Laura to sing "Nelly Grey." Do you know that, Elizabeth?

ELIZABETH (*going to the piano*): Yes Ma'am.

LUCY: Do you know it, Laura?

LAURA (*joining her sister at the piano*): Yes Ma'am.

SARAH: Poor Cousin Gertrude Williams is back in the asylum.

MR. VAUGHN: I'm sorry to hear that.

SARAH: She tried to murder their cook. She thought she was poisoning her food.

MR. VAUGHN: Dr. Stone's boy is in the asylum, you know.

SARAH: Did he get violent?

MR. VAUGHN: No, he just stopped eating one day and then he sat in a chair and they couldn't get him to move. He wouldn't look at them, he wouldn't talk to them. He just sat.

LUCY: That's a cross.

MR. VAUGHN: Are you girls ready?

LAURA: Yes Sir.

(ELIZABETH *starts to play and* LAURA *sings "Nellie Grey."* LAURA *stops singing, she cries.*)

MRS. VAUGHN: What is it, Laura? Does the song affect you so? (*To the others:*) Laura is very tender-hearted. (*She goes to her.*) My goodness, Mr. Vaughn, the child is hysterical. The poor child is absolutely hysterical. (*She holds* LAURA.) Now . . . Now . . . Now . . . Sh . . . Sh . . . Sh . . . (MRS. VAUGHN *takes* LAURA *out.*)

SARAH: Billy's wife, Asa, was a Catholic, you know. She was born a Catholic and she died one, although she wasn't much of anything in between. They say she made a confession to the priest before she died. That's one I'd like to have heard. I bet that priest blushed listening to that confession.

LUCY: Why are you bringing up Asa?

SARAH: Just thought about her. I've been thinking about her ever since yesterday when the train passed by their plantation. Is she buried out there?

MR. VAUGHN: Yes, she is.

(MRS. VAUGHN *and* LAURA *re-enter.*)

MRS. VAUGHN: Elizabeth, will you play for us now?

SARAH: I want to go out there sometime and visit her grave.

MR. VAUGHN: Why?

SARAH: I love to visit graveyards. I like to see what they put on people's tombstones. What in the world would you put on Asa's tombstone? What happened to that child, Iris, that she had up at her place so much towards the last?

MR. VAUGHN: She committed suicide.

SARAH: Did she? How?

MR. VAUGHN: She took poison. She had a horrible death.

SARAH: Mercy, Mercy!

(ELIZABETH *begins to play a piece.* HORACE ROBEDAUX *appears on the gallery and goes to front door. He knocks.* MR. VAUGHN *rises.*)

MR. VAUGHN: Excuse me. (*He goes out.*)

SARAH: You know why Gertrude goes off that way? Because her mother and father were first cousins. That's taking a chance.

MR. VAUGHN (*coming onto the porch*): Yes? Oh, hello, Horace.

HORACE: Is Elizabeth home?

MR. VAUGHN: Yes.

HORACE: May I see her please?

(MR. VAUGHN *looks at him. He has on a tux. He starts to question him, but decides not to and goes.* ELIZABETH *continues to play.* MR. VAUGHN *comes in.*)

MR. VAUGHN: Elizabeth . . .

ELIZABETH: Yes?

MR. VAUGHN: There is someone to see you.

ELIZABETH: Who, Papa?

MR. VAUGHN: Horace Robedaux.

ELIZABETH: Yes Sir. Thank you. (*She goes.*)

MRS. VAUGHN: What's he doing here this time of night?

MR. VAUGHN: God knows. He has on a tuxedo.

MRS. VAUGHN: A tuxedo?

MR. VAUGHN: Yes. He looks like a fool standing there in a tuxedo.

MRS. VAUGHN: I hope he doesn't start calling on her.

SARAH: Don't you like his family?

MRS. VAUGHN: Yes. I like his family. They are all friends of mine.

MR. VAUGHN: We don't like him.

MRS. VAUGHN: He's not the kind of young man we want her to see.

MR. VAUGHN: I don't want her to see any young men. Laura either. They have all they need, both of them. I can take care of them perfectly well.

LUCY: You won't be here forever, Henry . . .

MR. VAUGHN: Never mind . . . I'll leave the money to take care of them.

LAURA: I'm not going to be an old maid. I tell you that.

MR. VAUGHN: Be quiet. You don't know what you are talking about.

(ELIZABETH *comes out to the porch.* HORACE *goes to her.*)

ELIZABETH: Hello, Horace. What are you doing here? I thought you were at the dance.

HORACE: I wasn't having a good time without you. I hope it was all right my coming here in my tuxedo. Your father didn't seem very pleased to see me. (*Pause.*) I suppose I should call first.

ELIZABETH: Maybe you should, Horace.

HORACE: Can you go for a walk with me?

ELIZABETH: Where to?

HORACE: I thought we'd walk uptown and get some ice cream.

ELIZABETH: I'll see.

(*She goes in.* LAURA *has been playing a piece on the piano.* ELIZABETH *comes in.*)

ELIZABETH: Papa . . .

MR. VAUGHN: Sh . . . We're listening to your sister play.

ELIZABETH (*waiting until the piece is finished*): Papa, may I go for a walk?

MR. VAUGHN: Where to?

ELIZABETH: Uptown to get some ice cream.

MR. VAUGHN: I don't think so. Not this time of night.

ELIZABETH: Papa, please . . .

MR. VAUGHN: No, Elizabeth.

MRS. VAUGHN: Why isn't he at the dance?

ELIZABETH: He wasn't having a good time.

MR. VAUGHN: Well, tell him for me I think he looks like a fool walking around town in a tuxedo.

ELIZABETH: Papa . . .

MR. VAUGHN: No, Elizabeth.

(She leaves.)

MRS. VAUGHN: It's always something to drive you crazy.

SARAH: What does he do?

MR. VAUGHN: He's a traveling man.

SARAH: Oh, my God! They are the worst kind. You remember Cousin Amie Sprague married a traveling man and he almost drove her crazy. She died of a broken heart. Poor thing! Oh, I pity you if she marries a traveling man.

LUCY: Nobody is talking about her marrying anybody, Sarah. One good thing about a traveling man is he'll be away a lot and she'll get bored and go out with other young men.

MR. VAUGHN: I don't want her to go out with other young men. I don't want my girls to go out with anybody.

LAURA: I'm not going to be an old maid.

MR. VAUGHN: You be quiet, Laura. Don't talk smarty.

SARAH: I'm an old maid, honey. There are worse things in this world.

LUCY: Well, I think I'll go up to my room. Are you coming, Sarah?

SARAH: Yes, I'll join you.

MRS. VAUGHN: I think I'm about ready for bed myself.

(LUCY, SARAH, MRS. VAUGHN _and_ LAURA _exit._ MR. VAUGHN
looks out the window at HORACE _on the gallery._ MR. VAUGHN _leaves
the window._ ELIZABETH _comes back onto the gallery from the house.
A couple dances in and out._ ELIZABETH _goes to_ HORACE.)

ELIZABETH: I can't go.

HORACE: Why?

ELIZABETH: My father doesn't want me to. (_Pause._) Were
there a lot of people at the dance?

HORACE: A good crowd.

ELIZABETH: Was it a nice orchestra?

HORACE: Yes. (_Pause._) I have to leave again day after tomorrow. I start my new territory then.

ELIZABETH: Where do you go to?

HORACE: I start out in East Texas. I work my way over to
Arkansas. (_Pause._) You haven't forgotten our date tomorrow night?

ELIZABETH: No.

HORACE: May I come and see you the next night, too?

ELIZABETH: I have choir practice the next night.

HORACE: May I walk you over to choir practice and then
back home?

ELIZABETH: I guess so.

(MR. VAUGHN _shuts off light in music room, and leaves._)

HORACE: Someone told my aunt Mr. Vaughn has said he
didn't like me.

ELIZABETH: Who told your aunt that?

HORACE: She wouldn't say.

ELIZABETH: I don't believe he said that.

HORACE: Do you think he likes me?

ELIZABETH: To tell you the truth, sometimes I think he doesn't want me to go with anyone or ever marry.

HORACE: He's married.

ELIZABETH: Yes.

HORACE: And happily married?

ELIZABETH: Yes.

HORACE: Then why?

ELIZABETH: I don't know.

(*A couple dances by.*)

HORACE: I love that piece the orchestra is playing. Why don't we dance?

ELIZABETH: Oh, I can't, thank you. Papa doesn't want me to dance.

HORACE: Not even here? On your own porch?

ELIZABETH: No.

(*A couple dances in and out.*)

He's never danced in his life. Mama used to as a girl, but she stopped when she married Papa.

HORACE: All my family dance.

ELIZABETH: I know they do.

HORACE: My aunt led the cake walk tonight.

ELIZABETH: I know. (*Pause.*) It's a lovely night, isn't it?

HORACE: Yes. (*Pause.*) Leo Theil and Sybil Thomas got married late this afternoon.

ELIZABETH: Did they?

HORACE: It was a very quick wedding. They got married at Sybil's house. They got married in such a hurry only one of her brothers was able to get here for it. Leo said he made up his mind to get married this morning. Of course, the talk around town is that Mr. Thomas's gun made up his mind for him.

(MR. VAUGHN *appears in front door.*)

MR. VAUGHN: Elizabeth, I think you had better come in now.

ELIZABETH: Why, Papa?

MR. VAUGHN: Because I asked you to.

ELIZABETH: Let me visit a few minutes longer.

MR. VAUGHN: Just a few minutes. I don't want to have to call you again. (*He goes.*)

HORACE: Why doesn't he like me?

ELIZABETH: Why do you think he doesn't like you?

HORACE: I can tell.

ELIZABETH: He's never told me he doesn't like you. He's that way with all the young men that come over.

HORACE: Someone told my aunt he didn't like me because I'm too wild. (*Pause.*) I'm not all that wild, Elizabeth.

ELIZABETH: You go with a very wild bunch of boys: Felix, Archie, Ed Landray, your cousins, the Harris boys, Lloyd Gallahow, Steve Tyler.

HORACE: They're my friends and cousins . . . They're the only boys here my age. They're the ones I grew up with.

ELIZABETH: Why are boys so wild?

HORACE: Girls can be wild, too.

ELIZABETH: My friends can be silly, but I don't think they're wild. (*Pause.*) Why did you stop seeing Dolly Weems?

HORACE: Because I like you now.

ELIZABETH: Does she know you're not going to see her any more?

HORACE: She knew that last summer. She's going with Felix now.

ELIZABETH: Did she start going with him after you broke up with her?

HORACE: I don't know.

ELIZABETH: Did you tell her why you didn't want to go with her any longer?

HORACE: No.

ELIZABETH: Do you go with girls on the road?

HORACE: Sometimes.

ELIZABETH: Nice girls?

HORACE: Yes.

ELIZABETH: How long will you be gone this time?

HORACE: Three months. I'll be home at Christmas.

ELIZABETH: For how long?

HORACE: Five days. I'll be here for the Christmas dance. I hope you'll go with me?

ELIZABETH: You know I'm not allowed to dance.

HORACE: We wouldn't dance. We'll just go and watch.

ELIZABETH: That wouldn't be any fun for you. You like to dance.

HORACE: I don't have to dance. I'd rather be with you.

ELIZABETH: Thank you.

HORACE: I'd rather be with you than any girl I've ever known.

ELIZABETH: That's very sweet. Thank you. I enjoy being with you, too.

HORACE: Thank you very much. Am I the first boy you've gone with?

ELIZABETH: No. I've had a few beaus. We'd go to church and the picture show. Sometimes boys come over and play the piano and sing songs.

HORACE: Did you ever go steady with a boy?

ELIZABETH: Yes. I thought everybody knew I did.

HORACE: Syd Joplin?

ELIZABETH: Yes.

HORACE: Were you in love with him?

ELIZABETH: I thought I was. I wanted to marry him.

HORACE: Why didn't you?

ELIZABETH: Papa forbid it. Syd wanted me to elope with him. I almost did.

HORACE: Why didn't you?

ELIZABETH: I was scared to. Papa and Mama said they would never speak to me if I married him.

HORACE: Did you think they meant it?

ELIZABETH: Yes, I did.

HORACE: Is that why you didn't marry him?

ELIZABETH: I guess so. I guess I also wasn't sure myself.

HORACE: If you had been sure . . . would you have eloped?

ELIZABETH: I guess so. If I were sure. How can you ever be sure? (*Pause.*) Syd is dead now.

HORACE: I heard.

ELIZABETH: He never married.

HORACE: When was the last time you heard from him?

ELIZABETH: The day before he left here. He wrote me twice after that. But I returned his letters. His sister said I broke his heart, but I don't think so. I hear he was going with a girl in El Campo when he died.

HORACE: Can I have a date every night when I'm here for Christmas?

ELIZABETH: Every night?

HORACE: Yes.

ELIZABETH: All right.

HORACE: Will you write to me while I'm gone?

ELIZABETH: I told you I would the other night.

HORACE: Do you promise to write every day?

ELIZABETH: I'll try. But you're not to write me every day, remember?

HORACE: I remember.

ELIZABETH (*taking a ring and a chain out of her dress*): I'm wearing the ring you gave me. I think it's a beautiful ring.

HORACE: Why don't you wear it on your finger?

ELIZABETH: I don't dare. (*She points toward the house.*) You know . . . (*Pause.*) How will I know where to write you on the road?

HORACE: My company has given me the list of hotels I'll be staying at. I'll bring it tomorrow.

ELIZABETH: Do you like traveling?

HORACE: Pretty well. I like it a lot when business is good. Do you remember Barsoty?

ELIZABETH: Yes.

HORACE: He travels too. I saw him once in Baton Rouge. We plan to meet in Vicksburg in a month.

ELIZABETH: Tell him hello for me.

HORACE: I will. (*Pause.*) My mother was eighteen when she married my father.

ELIZABETH: That's awfully young.

HORACE: Yes. I guess so.

ELIZABETH: My mother was twenty-six when she married. She was considered an old maid. She had to go out and work for her living. She was a governess on a plantation and then she came here to work as a secretary in the courthouse. That's where she met my father. He was County Treasurer. They were both born in Brazoria County, but they didn't know each other until they met here. My mother was born on a plantation on Oyster Creek. Her father was a planter. But he didn't prosper. My father came from East Columbia. His father died when he was twelve.

HORACE: My father died when I was twelve.

ELIZABETH: Yes, I know. Your mother lives in Houston.

HORACE: Yes. I don't like Houston. I like it better here.

ELIZABETH: Did you ever live in Houston?

HORACE: For four months while I went to business school.

ELIZABETH: Did you live with your mother?

HORACE: No. She's married again.

ELIZABETH: Oh, yes. Do you like her husband?

HORACE: He's very kind to her. My sister is crazy about him.

ELIZABETH: Does she live with them?

HORACE: She did until she married.

ELIZABETH: She married Will Kidder?

HORACE: Yes.

ELIZABETH: You like him?

HORACE: He's a hard worker. He's very ambitious. He brags a lot. But I guess that's all right. He has a lot of confidence in himself. (*Pause.*) That's a gift I wish I had. I don't have a great deal of confidence in myself.

ELIZABETH: You don't?

HORACE: No.

ELIZABETH: I would think you would need confidence in order to be a salesman.

HORACE: I'm trying to develop it. It's hard, though. I have a very good line of merchandise, though, and that helps.

ELIZABETH: You seem very confident to me.

HORACE: You inspire that feeling.

ELIZABETH: That's nice to hear.

HORACE: I don't always want to be a salesman. Someday I hope to be a merchant.

ELIZABETH: What kind?

HORACE: Dry goods. I've clerked in stores since I was twelve.

ELIZABETH: I remember you waiting on me when you worked at the Hub. Not everybody can work with Mr. Jackson, but you always seemed to get on with him.

HORACE: He was always very good to me. He loaned me the money to go to business school.

ELIZABETH: That was certainly very nice of him.

HORACE: He was born in Alabama.

ELIZABETH: I know.

HORACE: He married Miss Eula Edmonds from Alabama.

ELIZABETH: Eula Edmonds. They're very congenial.

HORACE: Yes, they are.

ELIZABETH: I don't have a great deal of confidence in my-self, either.

HORACE: You don't?

ELIZABETH: No. I'm really very timid.

HORACE: I knew that.

ELIZABETH: Did you?

HORACE: Oh, yes. Mr. Jackson said if I ever wanted to have my own store he would loan me the money.

ELIZABETH: That's very nice. Would you like your own business?

HORACE: Someday.

(*They kiss.*)

ELIZABETH: Did you attend your sister's wedding?

HORACE: No. I was in Mississippi at the time.

ELIZABETH: What time was Sybil Thomas married?

HORACE: I think around four this afternoon. Someone saw Mrs. Thomas uptown in the late morning shopping. They said she was buying the wedding dress. I'm not sure of that, of course.

(*The porch light comes on.* MR. VAUGHN *appears in the doorway.*)

ELIZABETH: There's Papa. You'd better go.

HORACE: Will I see you tomorrow night?

ELIZABETH: Yes.

HORACE: Good night.

ELIZABETH: Good night.

HORACE: What time shall I come for you tomorrow? The picture show starts at seven.

ELIZABETH: Six-thirty.

HORACE: Good night.

ELIZABETH: Good night.

(*He leaves.* MR. VAUGHN *comes out.*)

MR. VAUGHN: It's very mild out.

ELIZABETH: Yes.

MR. VAUGHN: Will Horace go back to the dance?

ELIZABETH: I don't know, Sir. I didn't ask him.

MR. VAUGHN: When does he go back to his job on the road?

ELIZABETH: Day after tomorrow.

MR. VAUGHN: Sis Lucy and Sis Sarah would like to ride out and see our farm tomorrow. Would you like to go with us?

ELIZABETH: What time will we be home?

MR. VAUGHN: It will be dark.

ELIZABETH: How dark?

MR. VAUGHN: After seven. Would you like to go?

ELIZABETH: No Sir. I have a date tomorrow night for the picture show.

MR. VAUGHN: What's playing at the picture show?

ELIZABETH: I don't know, Sir.

MR. VAUGHN: Who are you going with?

ELIZABETH: Horace. I have a date with him the next night too.

MR. VAUGHN: Isn't that your choir practice night?

ELIZABETH: Yes Sir. Horace will walk me to the church and back.

MR. VAUGHN: He's an Episcopalian.

ELIZABETH: Yes Sir.

MR. VAUGHN: Not that any of his family attend much. I don't think they are churchgoers. (*Pause.*) I hear Horace Robedaux is very dissipated, Elizabeth.

ELIZABETH: No Sir, he's not.

MR. VAUGHN: He drinks and he gambles.

ELIZABETH: I don't think a whole lot, Papa.

MR. VAUGHN: He goes out with those that do. He had whiskey on his breath tonight.

ELIZABETH: Oh, I don't think so.

MR. VAUGHN: I could smell it. I have a very keen nose. I don't want him coming around here with liquor on his breath.

ELIZABETH: Yes Sir. I'll tell him.

MR. VAUGHN: I'll tell him.

ELIZABETH: Please don't, Papa. He already thinks you don't like him.

MR. VAUGHN: I don't. I would prefer you to wait awhile before marrying. And I certainly could never have you . . .

ELIZABETH: No one is talking about marriage, Papa. I've only had three dates in all.

MR. VAUGHN: Three too many. I would prefer you wouldn't see him again.

ELIZABETH: I already have a date with him tomorrow night, Papa. Remember we're going to the picture show.

MR. VAUGHN: You don't have to keep the date, Elizabeth. There is no law that says you have to do that. (*Pause.*) Laura said you heard about Syd Joplin's death?

ELIZABETH: Yes Sir, I did.

MR. VAUGHN: I think I was right about him, Elizabeth. It would have been a tragedy if you had married him.

ELIZABETH: Yes Sir.

MR. VAUGHN: You thought I was very cruel at the time. But you agree now I was right . . . Don't you?

ELIZABETH: Yes Sir.

MR. VAUGHN: You would have had a miserable life with him, Elizabeth. He couldn't keep a job. He had four jobs after he left here. (*Pause.*) If your Uncle Billy had listened to me about that last marriage of his, I believe he would have been alive today. I said to him: "Billy, didn't your first marriage teach you anything?" Stella, you know, was a vain, extravagant, foolish woman . . . a flirt. I don't say she was unfaithful, but at one time I thought so. But Billy, of all men, needed a wife who was steady and a home-maker. I couldn't understand how he could turn right around after that first marriage and marry Asa Davis. One look at her and you knew what she was. "Billy," I said, "Have you lost your mind?" But he didn't listen. He was sorry, too. He was a proud man, you know. And it was difficult for him to admit a mistake, but once after Asa had done one of those insane things she did to humiliate him, he came over here and he sat on the porch and he said, "Henry, I am miserable. I wish I had listened to you. She humiliates me constantly. She is unfaithful, she is drunk most of the time." And then he started drinking. And they were drunk together. He lost his law prac-tice. (*Pause.*) Oh, well, I know when you're young you think nothing like that can ever happen to me. Nothing. (*Pause.*) Your aunt wants you to come to Galveston and have a long visit. She wants you to stay until spring. She wants you to spend Christmas with her.

ELIZABETH: I can't be there for Christmas, Papa.

MR. VAUGHN: Why?

ELIZABETH: Horace will be back for Christmas. I told him I would see him then.

(*Pause.*)

MR. VAUGHN: You're interested in him then?

ELIZABETH: I think so.

MR. VAUGHN: After three dates?

ELIZABETH: We've known each other all our lives.

MR. VAUGHN: And he's interested in you?

ELIZABETH: I think so.

MR. VAUGHN: It's infatuation, Elizabeth, pure and simple. Don't indulge in it. Remember Syd Joplin. You said you could not live without him. (*Pause.*) Do you remember telling me that? (*Pause.*) You were sobbing and crying so, I thought you would surely be sick. (*Pause.*) Do you remember that?

ELIZABETH: Yes Sir.

MR. VAUGHN: Even your mother thought I had gone too far in my opposition and yet three days after he left here, it seemed to me you had forgotten all about him. Was that right?

ELIZABETH: Not all about him.

MR. VAUGHN: But you were glad you hadn't married him. You were glad I prevented it. (*Pause.*) Weren't you?

ELIZABETH: Yes Sir.

MR. VAUGHN: Horace has had a miserable life. I'm not blaming him for that, but he's drifted around, never having any discipline . . . living where he wants to . . . moving on when he wants to. He's never had any authority exercised over him at all. Actually, considering everything, he has done pretty well . . . Still . . .

ELIZABETH: What kind of man would you like me to marry, Papa?

MR. VAUGHN: Someone . . . anyone . . . that I feel could provide for you. That was reliable, sober, steady . . . Of

course I don't know why you and your sister feel this
need to rush into marriage. I give you everything; you had
two years of college. I would have sent you to a four year
college if you had wanted to go. I'm sending your sister
to Virginia to college next year. You have an excellent
musical education now. You can support yourself teaching music. (*Pause.*) So for heaven's sakes take your time
about marrying, look around, visit Galveston. I want to
send you to Virginia for a nice trip while Laura's in school
there.

ELIZABETH: You're happily married, Papa.

MR. VAUGHN: Yes, I am.

ELIZABETH: And Mama is certainly happy.

MR. VAUGHN: I think she is. We've been very fortunate.
We were older when we married . . . We . . . (*Pause.*) We're
happy. We are blessed with you children. (*Pause.*) Of
course there were times of despair and unhappiness when
we lost the other children . . . Still . . . (*Pause.*) How have
we been so fortunate? I guess that's what concerns us. We
look around at others. Billy, your mother's sisters, none
of them happily married.

ELIZABETH: None of them?

MR. VAUGHN: No. Your mother wouldn't like me telling
you, but you're grown now . . . and their marriages are
miserable. They all married for security and none of their
husbands have amounted to anything. That's what I think
you don't understand. You don't know what it is to do
without. Not to have food or clothes and what is worse
to have a house full of children that you can't half take
care of. When my father died so suddenly there was no
money. We were at the mercy of cousins and aunts and
uncles until I could get a job paying just enough to buy
us groceries. All around me I see poor, pitiful women,

half-starving, trying to make do, feed seven or eight children on the few dollars their trifling husbands have left over after their drinks. Or widowed at thirty or thirty-two . . . no way to earn any money and having to pass the children around to uncaring relatives. (*Pause.*) But none of that seems real to you, I suppose. You think, I'm sure you think, that will never happen to me. (Mrs. VAUGHN *comes out. To* Mrs. VAUGHN:) Elizabeth and I have been having a little talk. Where are Sis Lucy and Sis Sarah?

Mrs. VAUGHN: They've gone to bed. I just heard some very sad news. The Thomas girl that had to get married to the Theil boy went into labor at six o'clock this afternoon. This was their wedding day, you know. Evidently she was much further along in her pregnancy than she had told them. She was almost six months pregnant they think now. But she had been constantly trying to disguise her shape by corseting herself and evidently this brought on the labor. She was stricken late this afternoon and they feared at first for her life, but she's all right now.

ELIZABETH: Did she have the baby?

Mrs. VAUGHN: Yes, but it was born dead. They're burying it tomorrow in the afternoon. (*Pause.*) I don't know why hearing about it upset your sister so. Laura and Sybil weren't close were they? She is four years older than Laura. But she just sobbed and cried when I told her about it.

MR. VAUGHN: Elizabeth and I were discussing marriage. She seemed surprised when I told her your sisters' marriages were not happy.

Mrs. VAUGHN: And neither was your sister's. She married a man twenty years older, who died and left her with four children to care for.

ELIZABETH: Was she in love with Cousin Irvin?

MRS. VAUGHN: Ask your father. She's his sister.

MR. VAUGHN: Yes, she was. At least we all thought so.

ELIZABETH: And did she wait for him every afternoon at four o'clock?

MR. VAUGHN: What?

ELIZABETH: Nothing. It's not important. I just heard . . .

MR. VAUGHN: That he passed Mama's house every day at four. Or at least that's what Sarah reported to me. I never saw it. My sister and I have never discussed it.

MRS. VAUGHN: My sisters, of course, have never been widowed, but they have difficult lives. They all married for security and . . .

ELIZABETH: You didn't marry Papa for security?

MRS. VAUGHN: No, I didn't. I knew he was a hard worker, but I married him because I loved him and because I thought he loved me. My sisters . . . well . . .

(LAURA *comes out of the house, obviously very upset.*)

Laura, what is it?

LAURA: Mrs. Cookenboo called. Sybil Thomas just died.

MRS. VAUGHN: She's gotten it wrong. She gets everything wrong. It was the baby that died. Sybil is alive.

LAURA: No Ma'am. She said Sybil died.

MRS. VAUGHN: Oh, heavens! I'd better call someone to make sure.

(*She goes in. A couple dances in and out.*)

MR. VAUGHN: Are they going to dance all night?

ELIZABETH: It is not eleven yet, Papa. They always dance until midnight.

MR. VAUGHN: I'm going to bed. I think you both should be in bed too.

ELIZABETH: I'll be there directly.

(MR. VAUGHN *goes.*)

LAURA: I have to tell you something. I know how to dance too. I learned this year at school. (*Pause.*) And I have to tell you this . . . Last night when I spent the night over at Annie Gayle's, we slipped out too.

ELIZABETH: Who with?

LAURA: Ray Stanford and Mike Neal.

ELIZABETH: Where did you go?

LAURA: We just walked around the block twice. We saw Henry Kurtz coming home drunk, but he was so drunk he didn't even notice us.

MRS. VAUGHN (*coming out*): Mrs. Cookenboo was wrong. She always gets things wrong.

ELIZABETH: How did you find out?

MRS. VAUGHN: I called Mrs. Grey, Mrs. Thomas's sister. She had just come from the Thomas's and had talked to Sybil. She said she was feeling all right. Sad, of course, over losing the baby.

LAURA: Did you call Mrs. Cookenboo and tell her? She shouldn't be spreading stories like that around.

MRS. VAUGHN: Yes, I did. She argued with me, of course, like she always does. She claims to be the final authority on all that happens here. (*Pause.*) She told me something that I hope is not true. But if it is true I want you to tell me. If you both tell me the truth I promise I won't discuss it with your papa. If you both give me your solemn word that it will never happen again. (*Pause.*) She said that you, Elizabeth, had been seen several nights ago riding in a buggy with Rita, Horace Robedaux and Addis Miller. Is that true?

ELIZABETH: Yes Ma'am.

MRS. VAUGHN: Did Mrs. Carson give you permission to do this?

ELIZABETH: No Ma'am.

MRS. VAUGHN: Where did you tell her you were going when you left the house?

ELIZABETH: She didn't know we left.

MRS. VAUGHN: Where was she?

ELIZABETH: She was asleep.

MRS. VAUGHN: Then you slipped out?

ELIZABETH: We didn't slip out. We walked out.

MRS. VAUGHN: Don't be insolent with me, young lady. I'll call your papa out here in a second if you try acting like that with me. (*Pause.*) Who suggested this escapade? (*Pause.*) Was it you? (*No answer.*) Was it Rita? (*No answer.*) Was it Horace? Was it Addis?

ELIZABETH: No one suggested it. It just happened.

MRS. VAUGHN: Well, think about poor Sybil Thomas the next time you start slipping around with boys in a buggy in the middle of the night. Is this the first time you have done this?

ELIZABETH: Yes.

Mrs. Vaughn: Yes Ma'am . . . Elizabeth.

Elizabeth: I'm sorry. Yes Ma'am.

Mrs. Vaughn: Mrs. Cookenboo tells me Rita slips out this way quite often. Does she?

Elizabeth: I don't know.

Mrs. Vaughn: Laura. (Laura *begins to cry.*) Now just stop crying, Laura.

Laura: Oh, I'm so sorry, Mama. I don't know what got into me to do what I did. I felt bad the whole time and so did Annie. We both said afterward we both felt so bad we didn't enjoy it at all.

Mrs. Vaughn: What possessed you?

Laura: I don't know. I don't know. I don't know.

Mrs. Vaughn: You were supposed to spend the night with Annie tomorrow, weren't you?

Laura: Yes Ma'am.

Mrs. Vaughn: Well, you can't now.

Laura: Yes Ma'am.

Mr. Vaughn (*coming out*): Mrs. Cookenboo called back. She said you were wrong. Sybil Thomas did die. Mrs. Grey left the house before she died. She hemorrhaged suddenly and died before they could get the doctor. She's walking over now to see Mrs. Thomas and she wanted to know if you and the girls wanted to walk over with her? She says half the town is over there.

Mrs. Vaughn: Oh, poor Mrs. Thomas. Poor Mrs. Thomas. I think it's better the girls stay here. Will you walk with me, Mr. Vaughn? I don't really want to walk over there with just Mrs. Cookenboo at this time of night.

Mr. Vaughn: All right.

(*They go out.* Laura *and* Elizabeth *are silent for a beat. A couple dances in and away.*)

Laura: Was Sybil Thomas older than you?

Elizabeth: Yes.

Laura: She wasn't in your crowd though.

Elizabeth: Sometimes.

Laura: Did you like her?

Elizabeth: She was always jolly and had a very sweet disposition.

Laura: I thought she was pretty. Didn't you?

Elizabeth: Yes, I did.

Laura: I think you're pretty, Elizabeth.

Elizabeth: Thank you.

Laura: I love the way you do your hair and the way you dress.

Elizabeth: Thank you.

Laura: Do you think I'm going to be pretty?

Elizabeth: I think you're lovely now.

Laura: If it wasn't for the scar on my throat.

Elizabeth: I don't even notice it.

Laura: I do. I'm very conscious of it.

Elizabeth: You're lucky to be alive.

Laura: Yes, I am. I guess they thought I would die. Do you remember it at all when I drank the carbolic acid?

ELIZABETH: Of course I do.

LAURA: I was two, wasn't I?

ELIZABETH: Yes. I remember hearing Mama scream when she discovered it. I remember Mama and Papa both yelling at the nurse for being so careless and letting you near the bottle of acid, and I remember Mama sitting by your bed, night and day nursing you. I remember Papa saying she would kill herself if she didn't get some rest.

LAURA: I try to forget the whole thing and just when I think I have, Mrs. Jordan will say to me, "We didn't expect you to live, honey. We thought for sure we were all going to your funeral." (*Pause.*) Do you ever think about dying?

ELIZABETH: Sometimes.

LAURA: I wonder why did the two little girls die and not us? Why are they out in the graveyard and we are here?

ELIZABETH: I don't know.

LAURA: You're not half listening to me. What are you thinking about?

ELIZABETH: I don't know.

LAURA: I bet I know what you're thinking about.

ELIZABETH: What?

LAURA: Horace Robedaux.

ELIZABETH: Maybe. (*Pause.*) I'm in love with him.

LAURA: How can you know that?

ELIZABETH: I know.

LAURA: How can you be sure of that?

ELIZABETH: I'm sure.

LAURA: I hope someday I can be sure of something like that.

ELIZABETH: You will be.

LAURA: Be careful though, Elizabeth. You were sure about Syd, but then you changed your mind. You could change your mind again. (*Pause.*) The dance music has stopped.

ELIZABETH: It stopped quite a while ago.

LAURA: I wonder why it stopped so early?

ELIZABETH: Maybe they heard about Sybil Thomas.

LAURA: Maybe they did. (*Pause.*) Does Horace know how you feel?

ELIZABETH: I don't know.

LAURA: Would you marry him if he asked you?

ELIZABETH: I don't know.

LAURA: You'd have to be engaged first, I suppose. Do you think Mama would let you be engaged to him?

ELIZABETH: I think Mama might, but Papa wouldn't.

LAURA: Do you think you would have to elope to marry him?

ELIZABETH: Yes.

LAURA: Would you?

ELIZABETH: Yes.

LAURA: Even if it meant Mama and Papa never would forgive you?

ELIZABETH: Yes.

LAURA: Don't say that.

ELIZABETH: I mean it.

LAURA: Fifer Ecker's Mama and Papa never forgave her for eloping and her husband deserted her and she died all alone, in New Orleans. What if that happened to you?

ELIZABETH: I don't think it will happen to me. Not if I marry Horace. I don't think Horace would ever desert me. I think we will live together a long time and that we will be very happy all our married life.

LAURA: How can you be sure?

ELIZABETH: Because I am sure.

LAURA: Suppose he doesn't love you and is just infatuated and he meets someone out on the road while he's traveling around that he likes much better than you and he never asks you to marry him? What will you do then?

ELIZABETH: I don't know. I wouldn't know what I would do about that unless it happened. (*Pause.*) The other night when I was out riding with Horace he said he was not going to take out any other girls while he was away traveling this time. And I said I would not see any other young men. I said I would write to him at least three times a week, but I asked him not to write me but every ten days or so, because I didn't want Mama and Papa nagging me about it.

LAURA: If you're not seeing anyone else and he's not seeing anyone else, does that mean you're engaged?

ELIZABETH: In a way. (*She reaches into her dress and pulls out a ring that is around a chain. She shows it to* LAURA.) Look here.

LAURA: What's that?

ELIZABETH: It's a ring he gave me. I keep it hidden so Mama and Papa won't ask any questions.

LAURA: Is that an engagement ring?

ELIZABETH: I consider it so.

LAURA: And he must consider it so. I bet that's why he didn't take a date to the dance tonight and why he didn't dance when he got there. Because he thinks you're engaged. Oh, Elizabeth, I think it's terrible we have to deceive and slip around this way. Why can't we be like other girls and have our beaux come to the house and receive presents and go to the dances? I think we should just defy Papa and Mama and tell them right out.

ELIZABETH: I did that with Syd and it does no good. It just meant constant fighting. The boys won't come here because no one wants to be insulted.

LAURA: Of course with Syd it was a good thing they opposed your marrying him, because you didn't really love him.

ELIZABETH: No.

LAURA: Oh, my God! That worries me so. Suppose I think I'm in love with a man and I marry him and it turns out I'm not in love with him.

ELIZABETH: Oh, Laura, you'll go crazy if you always think of the bad things that can happen. I don't think of that.

LAURA: What do you think of?

ELIZABETH: I don't think.

LAURA: I wish to heaven I didn't. Everything bad that happens to a girl I begin to worry it will happen to me. All night I've been worrying. Part of the time I've been worrying that I'd end up an old maid like Aunt Sarah, and part of the time I worry that I'll fall in love with someone like Syd and defy Papa and run off with him and then realize I made a mistake and part of the time I worry . . . (*pause*) that what happened to Sybil Thomas will

happen to me and . . . (*pause*) could what happened to
Sybil Thomas ever happen to you? I don't mean the dying
part. I know we all have to die. I mean the other part
. . . having a baby before she was married. Do you think
she loved Leo? Do you think he loved her? Do you think
it was the only time she did? You know . . . (*Pause.*) Old
common Anna Landry said in the girls' room at school
that she did it whenever she wanted to and nothing ever
happened to her. And if it did she would get rid of it. How
do women do that?

ELIZABETH: Do what?

LAURA: Not have children if they don't want them?

ELIZABETH: I don't know.

LAURA: I guess we'll never know. I don't trust Anna Landry and I don't know who else to ask. Can you imagine
the expression on Mama's face, or Aunt Lucy's or
Mrs. Cookenboo's if I asked them something like that?
(*Pause.*) Anyway, even if I knew I would be afraid to do
something like that before I got married for fear God
would strike me dead. (*Pause.*) Aunt Sarah said that Sybil's
baby dying was God's punishment of her sin. Aunt Lucy
said if God punished sinners that way there would be a
lot of dead babies.

(HORACE *and* STEVE TYLER *enter the area.*)

HORACE: Steve and I were walking over to the Thomas's.
We saw you out here on the gallery. Did you hear about
Sybil?

ELIZABETH: Yes. We just feel terrible.

STEVE: I was at the dance. We were waltzing, and they
stopped the orchestra and they told us the sad news. Of
course, no one felt like dancing after that, so the orchestra

packed up and went home. I started for home too, and I saw old Horace sitting by himself in the Courthouse Square, and I said: "Horace, what are you doing out here in the Courthouse Square this time of night dressed in your tuxedo?" But I didn't have to ask him because one look at him told me he was lovesick. And we all know who he's lovesick about, too. She's not more than three feet away at this very moment and her name is not Laura.

HORACE: Steve, you have a big mouth. Where do you get all those ideas from?

STEVE: I know you, fellow. I know you like a book.

HORACE: Oh, sure.

STEVE: Sure . . . (*Pause.*) But we shouldn't be talking about such things with Sybil dead. I certainly meant no disrespect.

HORACE: Do you girls want to walk over to the Thomas's house? Steve says everyone that went to the dance is going by there to pay their respects.

ELIZABETH: We can't, thank you. Mama and Papa are over there with Mrs. Cookenboo.

STEVE: Did you hear when the funeral was going to be?

ELIZABETH: No.

STEVE: I guess they'll bury her at the same time they bury her baby. I bet it will be a big funeral. I bet everybody in town will go. Will you still be here for it, Horace?

HORACE: If they have it in the next two days. If not I'll be back on the road.

(*In the distance* AUNT CHARITY, *a black woman, is heard singing a hymn.*)

ELIZABETH: That's Aunt Charity going out to her house. She was in the kitchen late tonight. She had a lot of dishes for supper, I guess.

LAURA: She likes to take her time doing them she says.

(MR. *and* MRS. VAUGHN *come in.*)

ELIZABETH: Horace and Steve were on their way over to the Thomas's when they saw us on the gallery and came up to see if we wanted to go with them. May we?

MR. VAUGHN: No.

ELIZABETH: All the young people are going to pay their respects.

MR. VAUGHN: No. Don't you understand English, Elizabeth? N,O, NO!

HORACE: We'll be going along then. Good night. (*He and* STEVE *go.*)

ELIZABETH: Papa, why do you always have to be so rude? I asked you a civil question.

MR. VAUGHN: Which you surely knew the answer to.

ELIZABETH: And what if I did? What if I did? Do you have to always embarrass me in front of my friends? Do you want me sneaking around like Sybil Thomas? Is that what you want?

MRS. VAUGHN: Elizabeth!

ELIZABETH: Sometimes I think he won't be satisfied until something like that happens and he can say: "I told you so."

(*The chain with the ring breaks and falls on the floor.*)

MRS. VAUGHN: What's that?

ELIZABETH: It's nothing. (*She stoops to pick it up.*)

MRS. VAUGHN: What is it, Elizabeth?

ELIZABETH: It's a ring.

MRS. VAUGHN: Where did you get it?

ELIZABETH: From Horace.

MRS. VAUGHN: Why did he give it to you?

ELIZABETH: No reason.

MRS. VAUGHN: A boy gives a girl a ring for no reason? You mean he just handed you the ring without saying a word.

ELIZABETH: No. He said something . . .

MRS. VAUGHN: What did he say?

ELIZABETH: He said: "Will you wear this?"

MRS. VAUGHN: And what did you say?

ELIZABETH: I said I would.

MRS. VAUGHN: And why weren't you wearing it?

ELIZABETH: Because I was afraid.

MRS. VAUGHN: Of what?

ELIZABETH: Of what you and Papa would say. Of how you would act . . .

(*Pause.*)

MR. VAUGHN: I'm frightened for you, Elizabeth. Once you start practicing deceit there's no end to it. I want you to return the ring to him. (*He goes into the house.*)

LAURA: I guess everybody was very sad over at the Thomas's.

MRS. VAUGHN: Very sad.

LAURA: Did you see Sybil's body?

MRS. VAUGHN: No. They haven't brought her back yet from the undertakers. My heart is very heavy, girls. I hope this will end deceit in this house once and for all. (*She goes inside.*)

LAURA: Are you going to give Horace the ring back? (*Pause.*) Elizabeth? . . .

ELIZABETH: I heard you.

LAURA: Are you?

ELIZABETH: No.

LAURA: What will you do with it?

ELIZABETH: Give it to Allie or Rita to keep it for me.

LAURA: But what if they ask if you've returned it?

ELIZABETH: I'll say I have. (*Pause.*)

LAURA: Sister, I'm scared.

ELIZABETH: What of?

LAURA: I don't know. I'm scared we'll be punished some way.

ELIZABETH: What for?

LAURA: I don't know. But what are we to do? Be old maids? Do you think Mama was ever deceitful? Or Papa? I don't think they ever loved anyone else.

ELIZABETH: Papa did. He was engaged to a girl in East Columbia.

LAURA: What happened?

ELIZABETH: She was unfaithful to him.

LAURA: How?

ELIZABETH: I don't know. That's as much as I heard.

MRS. VAUGHN (*coming out*): I forgot to tell you, Elizabeth. Mrs. Thomas wants you to play for Sybil's funeral service. They are having all her friends sing in the choir. She said you would know all the hymns she was choosing. I said you would do it.

LAURA: When is the funeral?

MRS. VAUGHN: Friday. They have relatives coming from as far away as Mississippi. (*She cries.*) I'm afraid, girls. I'm so afraid that something will happen. I don't know how to make it clear to you . . . You've had very happy lives so far . . . You've always had everything you wanted. It can all be very different. How can I tell you? Some things are so difficult to talk about. I want to be honest with you both. I want you to be open with me. Your father is half sick with worry. He asked me to come have a talk with you. He thinks you both have questions you'd like to ask me. (*Pause.*) Do you? Laura? Elizabeth? Aren't there any questions?

LAURA: How did you know you were in love with Papa?

MRS. VAUGHN: I just did.

LAURA: How could you be sure?

MRS. VAUGHN: I just was. (*Pause.*) Elizabeth, do you have any questions?

ELIZABETH: No Ma'am.

LAURA: Elizabeth thought at one time she was in love with Syd Joplin. How come she wasn't?

MRS. VAUGHN: She was wrong.

LAURA: Why was she wrong?

MRS. VAUGHN: She just was. Just like I think one morning she is going to wake up and discover she is mistaken in how she thinks she feels about Horace Robedaux. (*To* Mr. Vaughn *as he comes out:*) Couldn't you sleep?

Mr. Vaughn: No.

Mrs. Vaughn: The girls and I have had a nice talk. I think they both realize we always have their best interest at heart. Don't you, girls? (*Pause.*) Oh, it's not easy, knowing what to do. What advice to give. What questions to ask. What questions to answer. (*Pause.*) It's just that we want the best for you both. Don't we, Mr. Vaughn?

Mr. Vaughn: Yes, we do.

Mrs. Vaughn: Why don't we have a party next week and invite some of the young people over? I think we should have more of the young people here in the house. Of course, we'll have to wait until after Sybil's funeral. Maybe we should even wait a week, but then I think it will be all right. Don't you, Mr. Vaughn?

Mr. Vaughn: Yes. I think it would be nice.

Mrs. Vaughn: I said to Mr. Vaughn, I refuse to worry. You've done one or two silly things. We all have. But you have good heads on your shoulders. You'll never do anything foolish, either of you. And I know we can trust you.

Elizabeth: Did Mrs. Thomas say what hymns she wanted played?

Mrs. Vaughn: What, Elizabeth?

Elizabeth: Did Mrs. Thomas say what hymns she wanted played?

Mrs. Vaughn: No, she didn't. She just said she was picking ones she was sure you'd know.

(*She goes.* Mr. Vaughn *goes.*)

ELIZABETH (*to herself*): I'm marrying Horace Robedaux . . . if he asks me.

MRS. VAUGHN (*reappearing*): Did you say something, Elizabeth?

ELIZABETH: No Ma'am.

MRS. VAUGHN: Oh, I thought you did. (*She goes.*)

ELIZABETH: I'm marrying Horace Robedaux.

LAURA: If he asks you.

ELIZABETH: If he asks me.

LAURA: And if he doesn't? Will you be an old maid? Or will you marry somebody else?

ELIZABETH: We'll see.

(*They are silent as the lights fade.*)

Valentine's Day

Characters

ELIZABETH ROBEDAUX
BESSIE STILLMAN
MR. GEORGE TYLER
BOBBY PATE
HORACE ROBEDAUX
RUTH AMOS
STEVE TYLER
MR. VAUGHN
MRS. VAUGHN
BROTHER VAUGHN

Act One

Scene 1

Christmas Eve, 1917

It is late afternoon. ELIZABETH *is in a rented room in the Pate house. There is a Christmas tree in the room; an empty baby crib, a double bed, a dresser and two chairs. She is five months pregnant. She is knitting a baby blanket.* BESSIE STILLMAN *knocks on the door.*

ELIZABETH: Come in.

BESSIE (*entering quietly*): Hello, Mary.

ELIZABETH: Elizabeth, honey. My name is Elizabeth. My mother's name is Mary . . .

BESSIE: I brought you a present and the baby a present.

ELIZABETH: Oh, thank you. There's a present for you, too, under the Christmas tree. (BESSIE *gets it.*) Sit down and visit, Bessie. (BESSIE *does so holding her present.*) I'm so glad you came by. I'm here all by myself. Mrs. Pate and Bobby have gone to Bay City for Christmas and Miss Ruth Amos and Horace are working late because of Christmas Eve.

(*There is a knock on the door.* ELIZABETH *opens it.* MR. GEORGE TYLER *is there.*)

ELIZABETH: Hello, Mr. George.

GEORGE: Is Horace here?

ELIZABETH: No Sir, he's still at the store.

GEORGE: What time do you expect him?

ELIZABETH: Not for awhile yet.

GEORGE: Tell him I was asking for him.

ELIZABETH: Yes Sir.

GEORGE: Merry Christmas. (*He goes.*)

BESSIE: Mr. George Tyler is off again, Mama says. Are you scared of him?

ELIZABETH: No. He looks harmless enough to me, poor thing.

BESSIE: Mama says he's gonna kill someone if they aren't careful. She says he's rich and kin to everybody in town and that's why everybody looks the other way no matter how he acts. He's not kin to me. Is he kin to you?

ELIZABETH: No. He's kin to Horace but only by marriage. This is the first Christmas Eve I've not spent with Mama and Papa, Bessie.

BESSIE: Is that so?

ELIZABETH: Yes, and last Christmas Eve was I think the most unhappy I'll ever know. At least, I hope I'll never know one more unhappy. Papa by then was so determined that I wasn't to marry and was so unpleasant and in such a bad temper anytime Horace came near the house that I finally asked Horace not to come any more. They sent me away to Virginia to visit my sister, Laura, in school there. And they sent me to Galveston in the summer to visit my aunts. Mama and Papa kept hoping if they could get me away long enough I would meet someone else and forget Horace. And then Allie Douglas married Hector and she was almost my closest friend. So Horace and I decided to run away and get married. The day before we were to elope my baby sister and a girlfriend were all busy making valentines and I pretended that's all I had on my mind, too. So I spent the whole day with them making valentines. I went to bed as soon as I could, but I couldn't sleep at all. I lay in bed listening to Mama and Papa in the next room talking. About that time a group of young men went over to Hazel and Nola Taylor's and began to serenade them. And then they left and it was quiet.

BESSIE: What songs did they play when they serenaded the Taylor girls?

ELIZABETH: I don't remember. I began to think of Clark Ferguson then, who was my closest friend. She was the first friend I had that died. She died in 1910 when she was sixteen. Do you remember Clark?

BESSIE: No.

ELIZABETH: Sure you do.

BESSIE: No Ma'am.

ELIZABETH: I don't see how anybody in this world that knew her could forget her.

BESSIE: I never knew her.

ELIZABETH: Oh, sure you knew her. You were bound to, but you've just forgotten is all. Anyway, I heard the Courthouse clock strike eleven and Mama and Papa were quiet and I figured they were asleep and I began to think of Clarkie, dying at sixteen, so pretty and sweet and here I was about to defy my parents and run off and marry and I began to cry. And I was sobbing so, I was afraid I would wake Mama and Papa or my sister, so I got out of bed and opened the window and looked out at the night. And I thought I'll never probably be looking out this window again until after I've married. I'll never be living in this house any more after tonight.

BESSIE: What is your papa's name?

ELIZABETH: Vaughn. Henry Vaughn. My mother is Mary. Maybe that's why you call me Mary. You get my first name mixed up with my mother's.

BESSIE: Did Clark Ferguson have black hair?

ELIZABETH: Yes.

BESSIE: And curls?

ELIZABETH: Yes.

BESSIE: Then I knew her.

ELIZABETH: Of course you did. We're going to Horace's Aunt Virgie's for Christmas. We'll open our presents tonight when he comes home. When do you open the presents at your house?

BESSIE: In the morning.

ELIZABETH: That's when we open them at our house, too.

(*There is a knock on the door.* ELIZABETH *goes and opens it.* MR. GEORGE TYLER *is there.*)

ELIZABETH: Mr. George?

GEORGE: Can you tell me how to get to town? I've forgotten.

ELIZABETH: Why, yes Sir. When you go outside the house you turn right.

GEORGE: Where is the train bridge?

ELIZABETH: That's to your left.

GEORGE: That's where the town used to be.

ELIZABETH: Yes Sir. I've heard that.

GEORGE: Before your time and mine.

ELIZABETH: Yes Sir.

GEORGE: They tell me you and Horace eloped.

ELIZABETH: Yes Sir.

GEORGE: And your mama and papa still haven't forgiven you?

ELIZABETH: No Sir.

GEORGE: I hear you slipped off to Allie and Hector's house for the wedding. .

ELIZABETH: Yes Sir.

GEORGE: And I heard the Methodist preacher refused to marry you out of friendship to Mr. Vaughn, and you and Horace then asked the Baptist preacher to marry you and he agreed, but first before the ceremony he said he wouldn't perform it unless you called your father and told him what you were about to do, and you phoned him and he begged you not to do it, he said you would live to regret it. Why do you think he made a statement like that?

ELIZABETH: I don't know, Sir.

GEORGE: And you were married on Valentine's Day?

ELIZABETH: Yes Sir. At one o'clock in the afternoon on Valentine's Day.

GEORGE: And I heard the Baptist preacher said he felt sure after it was done your mama and papa would forgive you and that he would personally call on them and intercede. Which I understand he did.

ELIZABETH: Yes Sir, he certainly did.

GEORGE: But I've heard tell it did no good because when they meet you uptown by accident they turn their heads and look the other way.

ELIZABETH: Yes Sir.

GEORGE: Isn't that pitiful? I'm sure sorry to hear that. I turn to the right?

ELIZABETH: Yes Sir.

GEORGE: How many blocks to town?

ELIZABETH: Two and a half.

(*He goes. She goes back to her room.* BESSIE *sings, half to herself, "Jingle Bells." There is a knock on the door.* ELIZABETH *goes. She opens it.* BOBBY PATE *is there. He is a small man and is very drunk.*)

BOBBY: Excuse me for disturbing you at this time of night, but I'm looking for my mother.

ELIZABETH: Oh, Mr. Bobby, she's gone to your brother's in Bay City.

BOBBY: Is this Christmas?

ELIZABETH: Christmas Eve.

BOBBY: Christmas Eve?

ELIZABETH: Yes.

BOBBY: What is the year, please?

ELIZABETH: 1917.

BOBBY: 1917? And we're at war?

ELIZABETH: Yes. I think your mother thought you were going with her to Bay City.

(BOBBY *leaves.*)

BOBBY (*offstage*): Mama . . . Mama . . .

(ELIZABETH *goes to the door and opens it.*)

ELIZABETH: She's not here, Mr. Bobby. She's gone to Bay City for Christmas.

BOBBY: Oh, yes. (*He looks around the room.*) What a pretty Christmas tree! May I come in and see it?

ELIZABETH: Why, certainly!

(*He comes inside and goes to the tree.*)

BOBBY: I don't believe we have a Christmas tree this year. I've been over all the house and I can't find it.

BESSIE: I hope to get what I want for Christmas. But I know I won't.

ELIZABETH: What do you want?

BESSIE: I want some more guinea pigs. Mama says I'm too old for them.

BOBBY: I was married to the sweetest girl, you know. She was quite a bit taller than me, but she was a real treasure. She left me, though. She couldn't stand the climate in this part of the country. "It rains so much here," she said, "it's a wonder you don't all have webbed feet." And one day I came home and she was gone. It was many years before I could find out where she went to or I would have gone after her and tried to get her back. She broke my heart. Mama says that's what I get for marrying beneath myself. She says it never works out. Mama says being born common is like a curse, you can't do nothing about it. "Well, common or not," I said, "I loved her." (*Pause.*) Where's Horace?

ELIZABETH: He's still working, Mr. Bobby.

BOBBY: That old boy works hard. He's always running someplace. Here, there. "What's he work so hard for?" Mama says. "To get into the good graces of Mr. Henry Vaughn," I told her. Mr. Henry Vaughn and his son drove by here as I was leaving home. His son drinks, you know. Drinks like a fish. "Does your papa know you drink that way, boy?" I asked him. "No," he said, "he'd kill me if he knew it."

BESSIE: Brother Vaughn is her brother.

BOBBY: Whose?

BESSIE (*pointing to* ELIZABETH): Mary's.

BOBBY: Oh, yes, that's right.

BESSIE: And Mr. Henry Vaughn is her father. And Mrs. Henry Vaughn is her mother. They don't speak to her because she eloped.

BOBBY: Oh, yes. That's true. I remember that now. (*Pause.*)

(MISS RUTH *and* HORACE *come in with packages.*)

MISS RUTH (*handing a package to* ELIZABETH): Merry Christmas!

ELIZABETH: Oh, thank you, Miss Ruth. Here's a little something for you, too. (*She reaches under the tree and gets her a present.*)

MISS RUTH: Thank you. What are you doing here, Mr. Bobby? Why aren't you in Bay City with your mother?

BOBBY: I've been here talking about old times. We've been reminiscing about old times.

(HORACE *kisses* ELIZABETH *and puts some packages under the tree.*)

ELIZABETH: Did Mr. George Tyler ever find you? He came here twice looking for you.

HORACE: I passed him on the way here and I said, "Merry Christmas, Cousin George." And he said merry Christmas to me but he said nothing about coming here.

BOBBY: When they wouldn't take me into the army I went down and tried to join the volunteers. They wouldn't have me either. Said I never stayed sober long enough to teach me anything. "Hell, Bobby," they said, "If we had to depend on you to guard this town from the Germans we'd be in a bad way." (*Pause.*) Do you think we're going to win this damn war, Horace?

(*A knock at the door.* HORACE *goes.* MR. GEORGE *is there.*)

HORACE: Oh, hello, Cousin George. Come in.

GEORGE: No, I can't stay. I'm on my way to church.

HORACE: This isn't Sunday, Cousin George.

GEORGE: What day is it?

HORACE: Tuesday. Christmas Eve.

GEORGE: Oh, yes. I came here to wish you a merry Christmas.

HORACE: Thank you. Merry Christmas to you, too.

(GEORGE *goes.* HORACE *goes to the window and looks out.*)

BOBBY: I bet Horace has lived in more houses than any of us. How many places have you stayed in, Horace?

HORACE: I couldn't begin to tell you. It would take me all night to remember them all.

BOBBY: Horace, Mama used to worry about you growing up. "Bobby, what is to become of that boy? He lives like an orphan," she'd say. "He's got no home." "Hell, Mama," I said, "He's no orphan. He's got a mama." "Where is she?" Mama asked. "Why isn't she here taking care of him?"

(HORACE *leaves the window.*)

ELIZABETH: Has he gone?

HORACE: Yes. Steve came and took him away.

BESSIE: Who's Steve?

MISS RUTH: His son.

BOBBY: Horace, how long has your daddy been dead?

HORACE: Let's see . . . Fifteen years.

BOBBY: Fifteen years. My daddy has been dead longer than that. I forget how long. I was a baby they say when he died.

MISS RUTH: You weren't a baby. You were a grown man.

BOBBY: I was?

MISS RUTH: Yes, indeed.

BOBBY: How old were you, Miss Elizabeth, when your father died?

ELIZABETH: He's not dead, Mr. Bobby. He's alive.

BOBBY: Oh, yes. That's right, but he doesn't speak to you.

ELIZABETH: No, he doesn't.

(*A knock at the door.* HORACE *goes.* STEVE TYLER, GEORGE'S *son, is there.*)

STEVE: Horace, Papa sent me in here to ask you over to the house later on tonight. He wants to have a long, private talk with you, he says.

HORACE: Steve, it's Christmas Eve. I've been working all day.

STEVE: I told Papa that. He says to tell you it's life or death.

HORACE: All right. I'll come over.

STEVE: Thank you. (*He goes.*)

MISS RUTH: To tell you the truth I'd be afraid to go over there.

HORACE: I'm not at all afraid of him.

BESSIE (*singing*): Jingle Bells, Jingle Bells, Jingle all the way . . .

STEVE (*opening the door again*): Excuse me for disturbing you again, folks. But Papa is not himself tonight it seems. I guess the excitement of Christmas is all too much for him, anyway, Horace, he says he can wait now for that talk until after Christmas. Merry Christmas!

MISS RUTH: Merry Christmas, Steve.

HORACE: Merry Christmas!

ELIZABETH: Merry Christmas!

(STEVE *goes.*)

BESSIE (*singing*): Jingle Bells . . . Jingle Bells . . . Jingle all the way . . .

(*She continues singing as the lights fade.*)

Scene 2

The lights come up in the bedroom. It is Christmas morning. ELIZA-
BETH *is making the bed. The phone rings.* HORACE *is seated in the
chair watching her. He's in his pants and shirt sleeves. His tie and
coat are on the chair. She is in her nightgown and robe.*

HORACE: I'll get it, honey.

(He goes out. She continues making the bed, singing to herself. HOR-
ACE *comes running back into the room.)*

HORACE: It's for you. I think it's your mother.

ELIZABETH: Oh, heavens! *(She goes running out.* HORACE *begins
to put on his tie and coat.* ELIZABETH *comes back in.)* Well, it was.
It was Mama! She said, "Do you know who this is, Elizabeth?" And of course I did and I said, "Mama." And she
said, "Yes," and then she said, "Merry Christmas," and I
began to cry. And she began to cry and then she said,
"May we come over in a few minutes? We have a few
little presents for you." And I said, "Yes," and that was
it. *(She finishes making the bed.)* We have to get presents for
them some way. I'll just die if they come here with presents and we have nothing at all for them.

HORACE: We can't do anything about it now. The stores
are all closed.

ELIZABETH: Didn't you close up for Mr. Dickson last night?

HORACE: Yes.

ELIZABETH: Then you must have the keys to his store?

HORACE: That's right.

ELIZABETH: Hurry down and get something for Mama and
Papa and Brother.

HORACE: What shall I get them?

ELIZABETH: I don't know, Horace. I can't think. I'm too excited. Use your own judgement.

HORACE: I don't know what to get for them. Your papa doesn't smoke.

ELIZABETH: No. He likes big red bandana handkerchiefs. Get him two of those, and get Mama some toilet water and get Brother a linen handkerchief . . . Hurry . . .

(*He goes running out. She finishes making the bed and then begins to get dressed; just as she has finished putting on her dress* BESSIE *calls.*)

BESSIE (*offstage*): Mary . . . Mary . . .

ELIZABETH: Come on in, Bessie. Merry Christmas! I can't ask you to stay, because my mother just called and she and Papa are on their way here.

(BESSIE *comes in. She has a cage with two guinea pigs.*)

BESSIE (*holding up the cage*): I got my guinea pigs. Mama says she just said I was too old for guinea pigs to throw me off the track. Mama says she prefers guinea pigs to white rats. She said I had better not want any white rats, because I won't get them. (ELIZABETH *has finished the bed.*) Did you have a happy Christmas?

ELIZABETH: Oh, yes. (*She now begins to pick up around the room. There are opened presents and wrapping paper scattered about.*)

BESSIE: Mama didn't get a thing she wanted for Christmas. She said the housecoat Papa bought her was the ugliest thing she'd ever seen and she got so mad she threw it at him. I bought her a pair of bloomers and she said four of her could get inside them. So I have to return them and get a smaller size. Papa has a headache. He says he's never known a happy Christmas and this year is no exception.

(*There is a knock on the door.* ELIZABETH *goes to the door.* MISS RUTH *is there.*)

MISS RUTH: Is Horace here?

ELIZABETH: No. He's gone to get presents for my family. They just called to say they were coming over.

MISS RUTH: How nice. I wonder if when Horace gets back he could look in on Mr. Bobby. I think he's sick.

ELIZABETH: I wouldn't wonder. He was very drunk last night.

MISS RUTH: He is moaning so loudly and every now and again he lets out a scream.

(*There is a knock at the door.* ELIZABETH *goes.* GEORGE TYLER *is there.*)

GEORGE: Is Horace here?

ELIZABETH: No, Mr. George. He went to the store.

GEORGE: I brought him a little Christmas present.

ELIZABETH: Oh, thank you.

GEORGE: It's not much, you understand. Just a little remembrance.

ELIZABETH: That's very thoughtful.

HORACE (*entering*): Oh, Cousin George, merry Christmas!

GEORGE: Merry Christmas to you, too.

ELIZABETH: Mr. George brought you a present, Horace.

HORACE: That's very kind of you. Come in and see our tree.

GEORGE: No. No, no, I can't. Merry Christmas.

HORACE: Merry Christmas to you.

GEORGE: Horace, did you know your Aunt Mary and I were in love with each other, and if we had married you'd call me Uncle George instead of cousin? (*He leaves.*)

HORACE: Wasn't that nice? I'll open it later. I think it is a handkerchief.

MISS RUTH: Well, it's the thought that counts.

ELIZABETH: Was that true? About your Aunt Mary?

HORACE: I don't know. I got the presents.

ELIZABETH: Oh, good.

(*She takes them from him and opens them. There are two red bandana handkerchiefs, two white linen handkerchiefs and a bottle of cologne.*)

HORACE: Brother's handkerchiefs are initialed.

ELIZABETH: Oh, yes.

HORACE: I got *H* because Henry is his name, even though everyone calls him Brother.

ELIZABETH: That's what I would have done. (*She begins to wrap them in Christmas paper.*)

MISS RUTH: You didn't hear Mr. Bobby as you came in?

HORACE: No'm.

MISS RUTH: I was telling Elizabeth he kept me awake half the night with his moans. Will you come see to Mr. Bobby, please, Horace? I don't like to go in his room. Sometimes he sleeps without his clothes on. (*She exits.*)

ELIZABETH: Horace, take this trash out with you, too, please.

(HORACE *takes empty boxes and wrapping paper and carries them out.* ELIZABETH *has placed her mother, father and brother's packages under the Christmas tree. She now goes about straightening out the decora-*

tions on the tree. HORACE *comes in. From another direction* MISS
RUTH *can be heard singing "After the Ball."*)

BESSIE: There goes Miss Ruth practicing again for the soldiers' benefit performance.

(HORACE *opens the package from* GEORGE TYLER.)

HORACE: My God, look at this, Elizabeth! My God! My
God!

ELIZABETH: What is it?

HORACE: It's ten one-hundred dollar bills!

ELIZABETH: Mercy!

(*There is a knock at the door.* ELIZABETH *goes.* MR. *and* MRS.
VAUGHN *and* BROTHER *are there.* MRS. VAUGHN *is a slight, pretty
woman, stylishly dressed.* MR. VAUGHN *is balding, plump.* BROTHER
is in college military uniform. He carries the family packages.)

MRS. VAUGHN: Merry Christmas!

ELIZABETH: Merry Christmas! (*They embrace and then she goes
to her father.*) Merry Christmas, Papa! (*She embraces him. He
seems embarrassed and not at all sure of how to respond to her. She
goes to her brother and kisses him.*) Merry Christmas, Brother!

BROTHER: Merry Christmas, Sister!

(*He puts the presents under the tree.*)

ELIZABETH: My heavens, who is all that for?

BROTHER: Not all for you and your old man. There are
some presents for a future member of the family.

(HORACE *has been standing watching them, smiling self-consciously.*
MRS. VAUGHN *goes to him.*)

MRS. VAUGHN: Hello, Horace. Merry Christmas!

HORACE: Thank you. Merry Christmas to you, too! (*He goes to* MR. VAUGHN, *extending his hand.*) Merry Christmas, Mr. Vaughn!

MR. VAUGHN: Thank you. Merry Christmas to you, too.

ELIZABETH: I'm so embarrassed. I've never seen so many presents in my life. We just got simple things for you.

MRS. VAUGHN: They're mostly things for the baby. I see you have a crib already.

ELIZABETH: They had a sale last month and we decided to buy it then.

MRS. VAUGHN: I'm glad we didn't get one then. Do you have a buggy?

ELIZABETH: No.

MRS. VAUGHN: Then don't get one. Your papa and I have one put aside.

ELIZABETH: Oh, Mama.

(BROTHER *piles five of the presents in one corner.*)

BROTHER: These are all for the baby. (*He takes two presents and hands them to* ELIZABETH.) These are for you. (*And two more he hands to* HORACE.) And these are for you.

HORACE: Thank you.

ELIZABETH: Get their presents, Horace, please.

(*He does so. He hands one to* MRS. VAUGHN, *one to* BROTHER, *and one to* MR. VAUGHN.)

MRS. VAUGHN: Thank you.

(*Everyone opens their presents.* Elizabeth *has opened hers first. There is a nightgown in one and a negligee in another.*)

Elizabeth: Oh, how lovely!

Mrs. Vaughn: I thought you should have something pretty to wear when you stay in bed after you have the baby.

Brother: What do you want? A boy or a girl?

Elizabeth: I don't care, really.

Mrs. Vaughn (*opening her package of cologne*): This is very nice, thank you.

(Horace *hasopened his now. They have given him a tie and a shirt.*)

Elizabeth: Aren't they pretty?

Horace: They sure are. Thank you.

Mrs. Vaughn: I hope the shirt fits. Mr. Lewis said it would. It's a fifteen neck.

Horace: That's my size.

Mrs. Vaughn: And a thirty-four sleeve.

Horace: Perfect.

Mr. Vaughn (*opening his package and taking out his bandana handkerchiefs*): They're my favorites. Thank you. Can never have too many.

Brother (*opening his present*): Thanks. I can never have too many of these either. It's got my initial on it, too.

Elizabeth: How's college, Brother?

(*He makes a face.*)

MR. VAUGHN: He doesn't apply himself. I would have thought he should have learned at the Academy that you have to study if you want to make grades. But they were lenient at the Academy. A & M is not lenient. If he doesn't study and make his grades he will get kicked out.

MRS. VAUGHN: There were so many rich boys at Allen Academy. There was a great deal of gambling going on and carousing. I'm afraid Brother sometimes got the wrong idea of things. But his papa let him know that he wasn't going to be like the Darst boys' father and the Lee boys' and spend his life getting him out of scrapes. That if he makes his bed he has to lie in it. I think Brother understands that now. (MRS. VAUGHN *looks up and sees* BESSIE.) Why, Bessie! In all the confusion I didn't see you standing there. Merry Christmas!

BESSIE: Yes Ma'am. Merry Christmas! I have to go. (*She leaves.*)

HORACE: She's over here a lot. She's been a lot of company to Elizabeth.

MRS. VAUGHN: Mr. George Tyler is off again, they say. They can't get him to eat. He accuses his wife of poisoning his food. It's so sad for them all. He went running in the front yard late yesterday afternoon with no clothes on.

BROTHER: Naked?

MRS. VAUGHN: Naked. A fine Christmas they will have.

MR. VAUGHN: He's had these spells many times before, you know. They've tried to keep it quiet, but of course, they couldn't.

ELIZABETH: He just left here. He seemed all right to us. He brought Horace a Christmas present.

MRS. VAUGHN: Did he? What did he give you, Horace?

HORACE: Ten one-hundred dollar bills!

MRS. VAUGHN: My goodness! Wasn't that generous of him, Mr. Vaughn?

MR. VAUGHN: Yes.

ELIZABETH: Did you hear from Laura and Dora?

MRS. VAUGHN: Oh, yes. We got sweet letters from both of them. Their presents haven't arrived yet. But you know the mails at Christmas time. Nothing is ever on time.

MRS. VAUGHN: How's your mother, Horace?

HORACE: She's well, last I heard.

ELIZABETH: Horace's mother is not much of a letter writer.

MRS. VAUGHN: No? I never have met your stepfather. Have you met him, Elizabeth?

ELIZABETH: Oh, yes Ma'am. Right after we were married. We went down on the train to Houston and spent the Sunday with them.

BROTHER: I had a fine Christmas. I got twenty dollars from Papa and Mama, a set of military hairbrushes, cufflinks, a wristwatch, a muffler, and a pair of gloves.

ELIZABETH: Horace spoiled me to death. I got a nightgown from him too, a bottle of perfume, some bedroom slippers, and a subscription to *Holland's* magazine. We'll have a lot of Christmas this year. We opened our presents to each other last night and now your presents and this afternoon, his aunts'. (*To* HORACE:) Tell them what you got, sweetheart.

HORACE: A smoking jacket, a box of White Owl Cigars, and a subscription to the *Galveston News,* all from Elizabeth.

MRS. VAUGHN: Look what I got. (*She points to a handsome diamond bar pin pinned to her dress.*)

ELIZABETH: Oh, Mama! How beautiful!

BROTHER: It cost a lot of money.

MRS. VAUGHN: I'm sure it did.

BROTHER: I know what it cost.

MR. VAUGHN: How do you know?

BROTHER: I saw the price tag before you took it off.

ELIZABETH: What did you get, Papa?

MRS. VAUGHN: Nothing as handsome as this.

MR. VAUGHN: I'm pleased. An umbrella, which I badly needed, bedroom slippers, a nightshirt, socks, and a tie.

MRS. VAUGHN: What did your mama send you all?

HORACE: Ma'am?

MRS. VAUGHN: For Christmas?

ELIZABETH: Their presents haven't gotten here yet.

MRS. VAUGHN: They probably are sitting in the post office right now. They know, of course, about the baby?

ELIZABETH: Yes. I wrote them.

MRS. VAUGHN: I know they're pleased.

ELIZABETH: I'm sure they are, but they haven't written back yet. Like I said, they're not great letter writers.

MR. VAUGHN: I remember my brother, Billy, worrying so about you one Christmas, Horace, when you were a boy. You were out at his wife's uncle's plantation. As a matter of fact, I think I went out there Christmas Day to see about Billy, who was under the weather as usual, and you and I had a little talk.

HORACE: Yes Sir, we did.

MR. VAUGHN: I was very close to my brother, Billy, you know.

HORACE: Yes Sir. Elizabeth said you were.

MR. VAUGHN: He was very smart. It was tragic he died so young. I've always had hopes Brother would follow in his footsteps and study law.

BROTHER: Papa, I'm going to have to disappoint you, I'm afraid. I want to make a lot of money, like you have. Did you know, Horace, that before Mr. Galbraith killed Mr. Mason, and his bank was so unsteady because of all the money they had loaned the farmers during all the years they had so many crop failures . . .

MR. VAUGHN (*interrupting*): What's the point of your story, Brother?

BROTHER: The point of my story, Papa, is that the bank would have gone under with all that money owed it they couldn't collect, if you hadn't taken fifty thousand dollars of your money and given it to them to use. You ought to see how they act in that bank when Papa walks in. They just jump up and dance when they see him. I guess you both are planning to go to Mr. Galbraith's trial? That's going to be a good one. I'm sorry I can't be here for that.

HORACE: Where will you be, Brother?

BROTHER: Back at school.

HORACE: Oh, yes.

BROTHER: I bet two dollars yesterday Mr. Galbraith would be convicted and sent to the pen, and I tell you . . .

MR. VAUGHN (*interrupting*): You bet?

BROTHER: Sure, I did. Easiest two dollars I ever made. He's guilty. He shot Mr. Mason and killed him and they're going to send him to the pen.

MR. VAUGHN: I'm not discussing his guilt. I'm discussing your betting. I thought you had learned your lesson at Allen Academy? I thought you had given me your word when you were suspended from there never to gamble or wager again?

MRS. VAUGHN: Please, Mr. Vaughn, let's don't spoil our Christmas Day.

MR. VAUGHN: It's spoiled for me, thank you. To think he's not learned his lesson about gambling.

BROTHER: I have, Papa. I won't ever go near dice or cards. I swore to you I wouldn't, and I won't.

MR. VAUGHN: You can gamble without the use of dice or cards, you know.

BROTHER: My God! I'm sorry I mentioned it. I didn't mean a thing in the world by it. If I win I won't collect the bet. It was harmless, Papa. You know how you do. Someone says, I bet Mr. Galbraith gets free and someone else says he won't and you say he won't and someone else says, I bet you two dollars he will.

MR. VAUGHN: It sickens me to think of my son betting on something like that.

BROTHER: I wasn't betting, Papa. I told you. We were just saying what we thought would happen. We all know he's guilty and he's going to the pen. I won't take the two dollars if they try to pay me.

MRS. VAUGHN: Well, let's change the subject, for goodness sake. It's Christmas Day.

MISS RUTH (*entering*): I hate terribly to bother you all, but I'm sure Elizabeth and Horace have told you about poor Mr. Bobby.

MRS. VAUGHN: No.

MISS RUTH (*whispering*): He's d-r-u-n-k.

HORACE: Did you get the doctor?

MISS RUTH: Yes, but as you know he is so small and he feels he can't handle Mr. Bobby by himself. He needs two strong men to help hold him down while he gives him a hypodermic.

BROTHER: I'll help you, Horace.

(BOBBY *comes in.* HORACE *goes toward him.*)

HORACE: Merry Christmas!

BOBBY: I'm looking for my mother.

HORACE: She's in Bay City.

BOBBY: That's right. Is this Christmas?

HORACE: Yes.

BOBBY: What year is it?

HORACE: 1917.

BOBBY: And there's a war on?

HORACE: Yes.

BOBBY: Mr. Henry Vaughn wouldn't take me when I volunteered my services. He didn't think I was good enough to fight for my country.

MR. VAUGHN: That's not true, Bobby, you were certainly good enough, but you see we have certain physical standards . . . we . . .

BOBBY: Who are you?

MR. VAUGHN: Henry Vaughn.

BOBBY: Oh, yes.

MR. VAUGHN: And he did try to join several times and that's certainly commendable. It makes you sick the way some of them do anything to keep out of it.

BROTHER: Lonnie Bigelow shot his toe off to keep out of the army.

MR. VAUGHN: We can't be sure of that, Brother. It might just have been an accident.

BROTHER: It wasn't an accident. It was deliberate. Lonnie Bigelow told Steve Mason if losing one big toe didn't keep him out he'd shoot the other one off.

(DR. GOODHUE, *a small man, appears.*)

DR. GOODHUE: Oh, here you are, Bobby. I was worried. I went to your room and it was empty.

BOBBY: Who are you?

DR. GOODHUE: I'm Dr. Goodhue, Bobby, now you know who I am.

BOBBY: What do you want with me?

DR. GOODHUE: I want to give you something to quiet you and make you feel better. Maybe sleep a little.

BOBBY: You're not giving me anything. You're not making a dope fiend out of me. You made a dope fiend out of Harry Newsome sticking him with needles, but you ain't doing it to me.

DR. GOODHUE (*interrupting*): Now, Bobby, that's not true. You know it's not true.

BOBBY: Harry Newsome says it's true. He's a dope fiend and he says you're responsible.

DR. GOODHUE: Bobby . . . Bobby . . . You're drunk, you don't know what you're saying.

BOBBY: I know what I'm saying. (*Pause.*) I was in the saloon the night Raymond Happ came in. He walked over to Briggs, the saloon keeper, and he said: "I told you if you sold my daddy another bottle of whiskey, I'd kill you." And he took out a gun and killed him. Let him go free, too, because they said Mr. Briggs had made a drunkard of his daddy by selling him whiskey. They're going to free Mr. Galbraith, too. I bet Brother Vaughn forty dollars they would. That's forty dollars found.

DR. GOODHUE: I'm sure. (*He goes toward him.*) Come on with me now. (*He tries to take his arm.*)

BOBBY: Let go of me. You sonovabitch.

DR. GOODHUE: Bobby, there are ladies present. (*To* HORACE:) Horace, I'll need help.

HORACE (*going to* BOBBY): Bobby . . . Mr. Bobby. Come with us now.

BOBBY: No. God damn you! No!

(BROTHER *comes up behind him and grabs him, pinning his arm.*)

BOBBY: Let go of me. You God damn sonovabitch! Let go of me! You drunken bastard! You're a drunk as much as I am.

BROTHER: Grab his feet, Horace.

(BOBBY *kicks and struggles but* HORACE *finally gets hold of his feet and they take him outside.* DR. GOODHUE *follows after them.* MR. VAUGHN *goes after them.*)

MISS RUTH: Isn't it sad? He's so gentlemanly, too, when he's sober. (*She goes.*)

MRS. VAUGHN: I hope your brother gets his eyes opened by this. Preaching doesn't do a bit of good, you know. But sometimes when they actually see something like this happening . . . (*Pause.*) Oh, Elizabeth, I'm worried about your brother. You heard what Mr. Bobby said about him just now.

ELIZABETH: He was drunk, Mama. He didn't know what he was saying.

(MR. VAUGHN *comes in.*)

MRS. VAUGHN: Have they quieted him?

MR. VAUGHN: They have just gotten him on the bed. He fights like a wild man.

MRS. VAUGHN: Your papa is working so hard, Elizabeth. Everyone calls on him when they need something done. When the bank reorganization is done, I am going to make him go with me to Mineral Wells and we'll take the baths for a week.

ELIZABETH: Please, don't ask Horace anymore about presents from his family. You know, I don't think they've ever exchanged gifts with him. He's extremely sensitive about it. I know this year he thought they would send something because he kept going to the post office and looking for something from them.

MRS. VAUGHN: Did he send them anything?

ELIZABETH: Yes, he did. He acted like he might not because, like he said, they had never exchanged presents, and I thought he wasn't going to. So I went down and bought a few things without telling him and sent them on and then he bought some things and sent them without saying anything to me. And Miss Virgie was in Houston last week and she saw his mother and she said she was very confused because she had gotten two boxes of presents. She told Miss Virgie she was worried about our being extravagant. She said it put her in a terrible position because his stepfather never sends anything to his people at Christmas, and she doesn't like to ask him for the money to buy presents for her people. I think he's a very strange man.

MRS. VAUGHN: The stepfather?

ELIZABETH: Yes. (*She whispers:*) I don't think Horace cares too much for him.

MRS. VAUGHN: I'm sorry.

ELIZABETH: They never come near him. And it hurts him, you know. I tell him it shouldn't, but it does.

MRS. VAUGHN: It would hurt me, wouldn't it hurt you, Mr. Vaughn?

MR. VAUGHN: I guess, but my God. He should be used to it by now. He's never had a home. Has he ever had a home?

MRS. VAUGHN: He has a home now.

MR. VAUGHN: This isn't a home. It's a rented room.

MRS. VAUGHN: I think it's very nice.

MR. VAUGHN: That may be, but it's still a rented room. A home is something you own, that belongs to you.

HORACE (*entering, exhausted*): He has the strength of ten men. He wore me out.

MR. VAUGHN: Did he give him the shot?

HORACE: Yes Sir.

MR. VAUGHN: Where is Brother?

HORACE: He's helping Miss Ruth find where Mr. Bobby has his whiskey hidden. She's afraid when the dope wears off he'll start to drink again unless they can find his bottle.

BROTHER (*entering*): Phone for you, Horace. (HORACE *goes.*) It was Steve Tyler. He said to wish you all a merry Christmas. He said his daddy was better now.

MRS. VAUGHN: I'm glad.

BROTHER: Mr. Bobby is wrong when he said I bet him forty dollars about Mr. Galbraith. I never said anything about forty dollars. It was two dollars, but I didn't correct him because drunk as he was, I knew it would just start an argument. (*He has a photograph. He hands it to his mother.*) Miss Ruth says this is a picture of his wife.

MRS. VAUGHN (*looking at it*): If it is, it's very flattering.

HORACE (*entering*): Steve says he's coming over to talk to me.

ELIZABETH: I wonder why he wants to talk to you.

HORACE: I don't know.

MR. VAUGHN (*rising*): We'd better be getting back home, Mary. It's almost time for our dinner. (*He starts out.* MRS. VAUGHN *puts the picture down.*)

MRS. VAUGHN: I'll call you, Elizabeth.

ELIZABETH: All right, Mama. (*They go out.*)

ELIZABETH (*to* HORACE): I'm so glad we've all made up.

HORACE: Yes.

ELIZABETH: That's the nicest Christmas present of all.

HORACE: Yes. (*Pause.*) I don't understand my mother or my sister. I would have thought they would have sent some kind of present to you at least . . . and the baby. I don't care about myself . . .

ELIZABETH: It doesn't matter to me.

HORACE: I wish I could say that, but it does matter to me. (*Pause.*) I'm ashamed of myself. But I felt such envy just now. I looked at your father and I thought: I envy him his success, his well-being, his affluence. And I envy his children having a father like that. Sending them to college. (*Pause.*) I don't understand your brother, not taking advantage of an education. Why, sometimes I think if I'd had someone help me get through high school and college my whole life might be different.

ELIZABETH: I think you've done very well. I am very proud of you. We've been married less than a year and you have money saved . . .

HORACE: I'm not complaining. I know I have a lot to be grateful for. But who isn't doing well now with a war on and the world needing our cotton and cotton selling at forty cents a pound? If one can't do well now, when can you? (*Pause.*) But suppose the war isn't over next year or the next and the unmarried men are all taken and they need more men and they draft those of us that have children? And I worry how long the few dollars I've been able to save will take care of you and the baby. (*Pause.*) Imagine being able to walk over to the bank like your father did and say, "Here's fifty thousand dollars. Use it to save your bank." (*Pause.*) God help me, Elizabeth, I'm jealous of your father. Forgive me.

(*Again in the distance,* MISS RUTH *sings "After the Ball."*)

HORACE: When I was nine I had some chickens that I raised as pets. They were the only pets I'd ever had and I loved them. They would eat out of my hand when I fed them and would follow me around the yard like dogs do their owners. Mama had a boarding house then and on the Christmas of my ninth year, she had no money to feed her boarders, so without telling me she went out back and killed my chickens for their Christmas dinner. (*Pause.*) When I found out I became ill. I had a raging fever for a week. They despaired for my life. Mama says the illness was never diagnosed. (*Pause.*) When I see her now she is all smiles and honey. She doesn't know the pain and the bitterness and the unhappiness she has caused me. Sometimes when I'm around her I have to walk out of the room to keep from telling her. I am no orphan, but I think of myself as an orphan, belonging to no one but you. I intend to have everything I didn't have before. A house of my own, some land, a yard, and in that yard I will plant growing things, fruitful things, fig trees, pecan trees, pear trees, peach trees . . . and I will have a garden and chickens. (*Pause.*) And I do believe I might now have these things, because you married me. I said to myself before our marriage, "She'll never marry you, no matter how much she says she loves you, because her father will stop it. He's a powerful man and he will prevail as he does in all ways." But he didn't stop us; you did marry me, and I tell you I've begun to know happiness for the first time in my life. I adore you. I worship you . . . and I thank you for marrying me. (*He holds her. There is a knock at the door.* HORACE *goes.*) Come in, Steve.

STEVE (*entering*): Was my father here earlier?

HORACE: Yes, he was.

STEVE: Did he give you a present? A Christmas present?

HORACE: Yes, he did.

STEVE: Was it money?

HORACE: Yes.

STEVE: My God! How much?

HORACE: Ten one-hundred dollar bills.

STEVE: My God! Mr. Jefferson, the president of the bank, called me an hour ago and said he had been worrying all day whether to tell me this or not; but when he heard Papa had gotten nervous again, he decided I should know. It seems day before yesterday he had drawn out fifteen thousand dollars in one-hundred dollar bills and had told the teller it was for Christmas presents for his colored friends. And the teller said he thought they were mighty lucky no matter what color they were. And he wondered if he knew any of the colored people and Daddy said you were one of them and the teller said I didn't know Horace Robedaux was colored and he said Daddy said he's not, but he's my cousin. The teller said he thought, of course, he wasn't making a great deal of sense. (HORACE *gives him the money.*) Oh, thank you. You don't know where else he went to?

HORACE: No, I don't.

STEVE: Well, I guess I'll have to go over to Freed Man's Town and see what I can find out. Merry Christmas to you both!

HORACE: Merry Christmas.

(STEVE *goes as the lights fade.*)

Scene 3

The lights come up in the bedroom. It's late afternoon, early January. ELIZABETH *is alone, knitting. There is a knock at the door. She opens the door.* BESSIE *is there.*

BESSIE: Mr. George Tyler is loose with a gun.

ELIZABETH: I know. He sent for Horace early this morning and said he knew he had done Horace's family a grave injustice, and he wanted him to ask them to forgive him, because he said he was in love with Horace's Aunt Mary and she was in love with him, but he broke her heart by marrying someone else. And he asked Horace how his Aunt Mary was and Horace told him she was dead and had been for twelve years and then Horace said Mr. George began to sob and cry and said no, he hadn't known she was dead and where was she buried since he had to go and visit her grave at once. And Horace said he was so unnerved at his carrying on like that that he couldn't remember where she was buried, he just knew it was someplace in West Texas, but he had the name of the town at the store and he told him he would go to the store right away and find it. No sooner had he gotten to the store than Steve called and asked what had he said to Mr. George to upset him so, and he explained about his telling him about his Aunt Mary being dead and Steve says is that why he's packing his bag and saying he's leaving right away for West Texas. And then we heard he'd slipped out of the house with a gun.

BESSIE: He's hiding down in the river bottoms. They say he is going to be hard to catch.

ELIZABETH: I imagine. He knows those river bottoms as well as anyone. He's hunted them all his life.

(In the distance MISS RUTH *sings "Lorena.")*

BESSIE: Miss Ruth is learning a new song. Mama said she did so well at the benefit she's learning another one in case she's asked to sing again. What kind of voice would you say that is?

ELIZABETH: A soprano.

BESSIE: Mama says it's hard to define. (*They listen to the song.*) Mama says Galli–Curci has nothing to worry about.

ELIZABETH (*picking up some house plans*): Look here, Bessie. Do you like this house?

BESSIE: Yes, I do. Whose is it?

ELIZABETH: I hope it's going to be mine, someday. Sooner than I ever expected. I got a note today in the mail from Papa saying Mama wanted to give me a house and to call him about it. And I did and he said she had in mind a house costing four thousand dollars, which is exactly what this costs. (*Pause.*) Oh, Bessie, I'm a nervous wreck! I want a house so badly to take the baby to. But I don't want to cross Horace. I don't know how he will feel taking something like this from Mama and Papa. (*Pause.*) I said to Papa when I talked to him, I said, "You know, Papa, Horace has almost saved enough money to build us a house." "I'm glad to hear it," he said, "then he can use that money to buy war bonds and help his country."

(*Again* MISS RUTH *sings "Lorena."*)

BESSIE: Well, Mr. Galbraith walked away a free man.

ELIZABETH: He's not free. He got a suspended sentence.

BESSIE: Yes Ma'am. But he didn't go to jail. I wonder if Mr. Bobby collected the forty dollars from your brother?

ELIZABETH: I don't know. Brother claims the bet was only for two.

HORACE (*entering*): They have Mr. George cornered down near the train bridge. They can see him and the sheriff is talking to him from the distance. They are not sure if he's armed or not. They're asking him if he's armed but he won't say. He said he's waiting down there for me.

ELIZABETH: Why is he waiting for you?

HORACE: He says I'm to bring him to where Aunt Mary is buried.

ELIZABETH: Are you going down there?

HORACE: I told the sheriff where she was buried, and the sheriff said to him I would take him if he gave himself up.

ELIZABETH: Will you?

HORACE: I guess I would, but they're just telling him that so he'll give himself up. I don't know if Cousin Sarah would want him visiting Aunt Mary's grave. (*He hands her a letter.*) This is from Mama. All she does is apologize, poor thing, for not having gotten us any Christmas presents.

ELIZABETH (*taking the letter and handing* HORACE *her father's note*): This came early this afternoon. (*He reads it.*) I called Papa. I told him you had almost saved the money for a house and he said you could use that money to buy war bonds.

HORACE: Do you think he believed I have the money almost saved to buy a house?

ELIZABETH: Why shouldn't he?

(MISS RUTH *sings "Lorena."*)

ELIZABETH: I told him we had plans for a house all picked out. He said he would be over at five to look at them.

HORACE: Did you tell him you would take his gift?

ELIZABETH: No. I thanked him, but I said I would first talk it over with you. He said to please tell you it was from Mama and not from him.

HORACE: If you take it the deed will be in your name. I don't want people here insinuating I married you for a house.

ELIZABETH: Who would say that?

HORACE: Everybody.

ELIZABETH: I won't take it, honey, if you don't want me to. It's just that I thought if we didn't use the money for the house, you could buy war bonds like Papa said or start your own store.

HORACE: Where is the house to be?

ELIZABETH: Right behind theirs. He's opening up that fifteen acres behind their house. He is giving the city permission to put a road through there.

HORACE: I don't mind your accepting it, if you make it clear that it is to be in your name and no part of it is to belong to me.

ELIZABETH: But it will be your home. I hope you'll always be able to think of it as your home.

HORACE: I'm sure I will. But I want everyone to understand who the gift was for.

ELIZABETH: They meant it for both of us.

HORACE: I don't think so. It says very clearly in the note: "Your mother wishes to give you a house."

ELIZABETH: Oh, Horace, please don't be sensitive. Our lives will be miserable if you are.

HORACE: I'm not, believe me. Even if it had been offered to both of us, I would insist that it be in your name.

GEORGE (*entering*): Horace . . .

HORACE: Oh, hello, Mr. George.

GEORGE: Is this your wife?

HORACE: Yes Sir. You know Elizabeth. She's Mr. Henry Vaughn's oldest daughter.

GEORGE: Oh, yes. (*Pointing to* BESSIE.) Is this your girl?

HORACE: No Sir. She lives down the street. She's just a neighbor.

GEORGE: Who does she belong to?

ELIZABETH: The Stillmans.

GEORGE: Are they new here?

ELIZABETH: They've been here about ten years.

GEORGE: Is this your house?

HORACE: No Sir. This is Mrs. Pate's house.

GEORGE: Where is Mrs. Pate? I'd like to say hello to her.

HORACE: She's not home. She's off with Mr. Bobby in Galveston. He's taking the Keeley Cure.

GEORGE: Is he drinking again?

HORACE: Yes Sir.

GEORGE: Isn't that too bad. Your daddy drank, son.

HORACE: Yes Sir.

GEORGE: It killed him.

HORACE: Yes Sir.

GEORGE: He was a close friend of mine, you know.

HORACE: Yes Sir.

GEORGE: I went to him. I said, "I've come to you as a friend. We all have troubles. Get hold of yourself for the sake of your baby son and little daughter . . . get hold of yourself." But my talking didn't do a bit of good. It never does, you know. I was just wasting my breath. He broke your mother's heart. How is your mother?

HORACE: She's well.

GEORGE: Your father sent for me before he died. Did I ever tell you this?

HORACE: No Sir.

GEORGE: He said: "George, I'm going to die. Promise me you'll look after my children. Promise me you'll never let them go hungry." (*Pause.*) I didn't keep my promise. And I'm sorry; I didn't keep my promise about a lot of things. (*Pause.*) You say Mary's dead?

HORACE: Yes Sir.

GEORGE: They won't let me die. I want to die and they've been chasing me all through the river bottoms. They give me no peace. First they want to kill me . . . my own wife tried to poison me and then when I want to take my own life they do all in their power to stop me. I've had a difficult life, you know, since I betrayed Mary. I've had no happiness. I've been punished unmercifully for what I've done. (*Pause.*) But I'm tired. Tired of running the river bottoms. Tired. (*Pause.*)

(MISS RUTH *sings "Lorena."*)

Do you know the way to my home?

HORACE: Yes Sir.

GEORGE: Will you take me there? I'm very confused. I tried to get there twice, but I'm confused.

HORACE: Yes Sir. (*They start out.* GEORGE *pauses.*)

GEORGE: How old was Mary when she died?

HORACE: I think she was forty.

GEORGE: She had long blonde hair when I last saw her. Did she when she died?

HORACE: I believe so.

GEORGE: Do you have a picture of her?

HORACE: No.

GEORGE: I married her cousin, you know, from Kentucky. What's her name?

HORACE: Sarah.

GEORGE: Oh, yes, Sarah Hendricks. She was from Louisville. Mary and her sister were all very musical. One played the piano, one the violin, one the guitar, one the banjo. Do you play a musical instrument?

HORACE: No Sir.

(GEORGE *starts out.* HORACE *follows him. Pause.* GEORGE *turns from the door.*)

GEORGE: Are you the son I had by Mary?

HORACE: No Sir.

GEORGE: Where is the son I had by Mary?

HORACE: I don't believe you had one by her, Sir.

GEORGE: I didn't?

HORACE: No Sir.

GEORGE: I have children?

HORACE: Yes Sir. You have four.

GEORGE: Did Mary ever have children?

HORACE: No Sir, she didn't.

GEORGE: Poor Mary. Dying without children. Your father worshipped you and your sister, you know. I remember the day your father died. I had been sitting up all night with him, waiting. And you were there and his brother and another friend. I forget his name . . .

HORACE: John Howard.

GEORGE: Oh, yes. John Howard. They think I'm crazy, you know. I do get terrible headaches, sometimes, and I can't think then, but I wouldn't harm anybody. Once I tried to kill Sarah, but I didn't mean it. I don't know why I did. I took a butcher knife on Christmas Eve and I chased her all around the house. I'm glad I didn't kill her. I would have been sorry if I had. I need help, you know. But nobody here can help me. I'm going out there now and I want you to go with me, son, and I want you to tell them for me I need help. And if I can't get it I want them to kill me, because I don't want to go on like this. Will you tell them that for me?

HORACE: Yes Sir.

GEORGE: Then let's go.

(*He goes out.* HORACE *follows after him.* BESSIE *moves to the window and watches.*)

ELIZABETH: Can you see them, Bessie?

BESSIE: Yes Ma'am. They're out in the yard. (*Pause.*)

ELIZABETH: Where are they now, Bessie?

BESSIE: They're going together down the street.

ELIZABETH: Are they talking together?

BESSIE: I believe so. He didn't sound crazy to me. I thought crazy people didn't make sense. Where is Miss Mary buried in West Texas?

ELIZABETH: Bandero.

BESSIE: Have you ever been there?

ELIZABETH: No.

BESSIE: Were you scared of him, Mary?

ELIZABETH: I don't know. It all happened so quickly.

(*There is a knock at the door.* MR. VAUGHN *comes in.*)

MR. VAUGHN: Was that Horace and Mr. George I saw going down the street?

ELIZABETH: Yes Sir. (*She goes to her father.*)

MR. VAUGHN: What is it, girl? You are trembling. Is Horace in danger?

ELIZABETH: No Sir. I don't think so. Oh, Papa. Mr. George is so pitiful. He doesn't know who his own wife is half the time.

MR. VAUGHN: You love your husband, don't you?

ELIZABETH: Yes, I do, Papa.

BESSIE: Goodbye, Mary. I'm going home.

ELIZABETH: Goodbye, Bessie.

(BESSIE *goes.*)

MR. VAUGHN: I wonder how he got past the sheriff and the others in the bottom and got in here.

ELIZABETH: He told Horace he wanted to get back home. He said he was confused as to how to get there. All he wants to talk about is Horace's Aunt Mary. Were they in love, Papa?

MR. VAUGHN: God knows. That must have been thirty years ago . . . At least . . . (*Pause.*) Anyway, he has four children by poor Miss Sarah. I expect she's wanted to go running through the river bottoms many a time. He hasn't been easy to live with even when he was his sanest. (*He sees the house plans.*) Are these the plans for the house? I got your brother's midterm report card today from college. It's just terrible. It couldn't be any worse. I have never seen such grades. What's to become of him? (*Pause. He looks again at the drawings.*) You say you can get this built for four thousand dollars?

ELIZABETH: Yes Sir.

MR. VAUGHN: Do you mind if I take it with me? And study it some.

ELIZABETH: No Sir.

(*He looks at his watch.*)

MR. VAUGHN: I'm just killing time waiting for the eight o'clock train from Houston. I have to wait for your mother. She went into Houston shopping. Did you have a chance to speak to Horace?

ELIZABETH: Yes Sir. He says it's all right with him as long as the house is put in my name. He doesn't want anyone here thinking he is taking help from you. I think he's awfully sensitive. (*Pause.*) He still doesn't think you like him, Papa.

MR. VAUGHN: I like him all right, Elizabeth. (*Pause.*) Give me time. These things take time.

ELIZABETH: Yes Sir.

MR. VAUGHN: We'll get used to each other before long. (*Pause.*) I sometimes think I should take your brother out of college. Put him on one of the farms. Let him learn how difficult it is for an uneducated man to earn a living. What do you think?

ELIZABETH: Oh, my God! I don't know, Papa!

MR. VAUGHN: And yet he's always had to work. I've seen to that. I tried not to spoil him. I was determined not to raise him like a rich man's son. But he's no ambition. None. And I hate to speak this way of my own child, but he's a terrible liar. You know that bet with Bobby Pate that he says was two dollars, and still swears it was? Bobby was right. It was forty dollars. There were four reliable witnesses that heard him make the bet. So I gave Bobby a check for the forty dollars today.

ELIZABETH: Maybe that's a mistake. Maybe if he had to pay the money himself . . .

MR. VAUGHN: Where is he going to get forty dollars going to A & M college? No. I paid it and I'll see to it he works at something around the house or the farm until I'm paid back. You know I'm not a very sociable man. It isn't just with Horace. I don't have an easy time talking with my own son.

ELIZABETH: Yes Sir. (*Pause.*) You see Horace's father died when he was twelve.

MR. VAUGHN: I was twelve when my father died. I went to work soon after, put myself through college.

ELIZABETH: I realize that, Papa.

MR. VAUGHN: I haven't stopped working for a second since I was twelve. (*Pause.*) I resented Horace. I resented him very much coming into my home and . . . (*Pause.*) But I'll get over it. Time heals all that.

(HORACE *comes in.* ELIZABETH *goes to him.*)

ELIZABETH: Oh, honey. I'm glad you're back. I was worrying. Did he go on home?

HORACE: I don't know. I only walked halfway with him when Steve and the sheriff drove up. Steve got out of the car and came over to us. He told Cousin George he was going to drive him home. I didn't think Cousin George would go with him at first, but finally he did and got into the car and drove away. I don't know where they will take him. You know it all happened so quickly that I forgot to tell Steve what Cousin George asked me to do, about needing help. Maybe I should go and find Steve and tell him that.

MR. VAUGHN: My God! You don't have to tell anybody that. He's needed help for years. Who can help him?

ELIZABETH: I showed Papa the plans for the house. He's taking them home to study them.

MR. VAUGHN: Tomorrow or the next day I'll drive you out and show you just where your two lots are to be and the new road. Unfortunately, I had to cut all the trees down on the land when I put in cotton except for two pecan trees, neither of which are on your lot. I'll show you where I think you should plant some trees. (*He goes.*)

ELIZABETH (*to* HORACE): You can do a a great deal on two lots. You can plant all the trees you want and you can have your chickens. (*She touches her stomach.*) I can feel the baby. Can you feel it?

HORACE (*touching her stomach*): Yes.

ELIZABETH: When I was three years old my baby sister, Jenny, died with diptheria. Mama was pregnant with Laura then and they had her in bed resting, and Papa's sisters from Brazoria came to take care of us and one of them took me in her arms to show me Jenny in her coffin and I got hysterical. I fought to get away and I raised such a commotion Papa ran in and his sister told him that he had an unnatural child that refused to look at her own dead sister. Mama doesn't even have Jenny's picture in the house any longer. It's hidden away at the bottom of her cedar chest. The day of Jenny's funeral they sent me away to play with a friend. My friend's older sister told me I was sent there because they didn't want me to see Jenny nailed up in a box and buried in the ground. Once when I was five and Laura was two I told her I wanted to show her where our dead sister was. Mama was off at the Missionary Society and the nurse looking after us had fallen asleep and we started to where I thought the grave-yard was. And Mr. Billy Lee, a friend of Papa's, saw us walking down the road and he asked where we were going and I said looking for our dead sister, and he said you can't find her, and I said why not, and he said because she's in heaven, and I said no she's not, she's shut up in a box and buried in the graveyard, and he put us both on his horse and took us out to the graveyard, and we found her grave with the little lamb on it. He said she's not there, she's in heaven, and I said who is there then, and he said no one. Well, I said, how did she get out of there, and he said God took her home with him.

BESSIE (*offstage*): Mary . . .

ELIZABETH: Yes, Bessie.

BESSIE (*entering*): Mr. George got away from them when they took him out of the car in front of the jailhouse. He started running back towards the river and then he stopped.

HORACE: Did they catch him again?

BESSIE: No Sir. He took out a knife and stabbed himself before they could get to him. He was dead by the time they got to him.

ELIZABETH: Poor thing.

BESSIE: I saw Mr. Bobby down there, too. He is drunk. Miss Ruth told me he slipped away from his mother in Galveston and got drunk and came on back here. Mrs. Pate is coming tonight on the eleven o'clock train.

(MISS RUTH *sings "Lorena."*)

HORACE: I guess I'd better go over to Cousin Sarah's and see if there is anything I can do.

ELIZABETH: What about your supper?

HORACE: I'll eat something uptown. You go on and eat without me. (*He goes.*)

ELIZABETH (*sits down, gets up, goes to window and calls*): Horace, come back. Don't leave me. (*Pause.*)

BESSIE: Did he hear you?

ELIZABETH: No.

BESSIE: Want me to fetch him back?

ELIZABETH: No.

(*Pause.* MISS RUTH *continues to sing "Lorena."*)

BESSIE: I told Mama about Miss Mary being buried in Bandero, Texas and she said it was Junction, as near as she could remember. She says it's just desolate out there. Do you think they'll bury him out there next to Miss Mary?

ELIZABETH: Oh, I doubt it.

BESSIE: Will they bury him here?

ELIZABETH: I would think so.

BESSIE: Aren't you going to eat your supper?

ELIZABETH: No. Not tonight. I'm not hungry now. (*Pause.*)

BESSIE: Are you mad at Horace because he went off without you?

ELIZABETH: No.

BESSIE: You're upset about something, though, aren't you?

ELIZABETH: Yes. Mr. George Tyler. I can't believe he was just here and now . . .

BESSIE: In two and a half weeks it's going to be Valentine's Day and you will have been married a year. Are you glad you married Horace?

ELIZABETH: Oh, yes. I am.

BESSIE: Do you love him now as much as when you married him?

ELIZABETH: Yes.

BESSIE: Do you think in twenty-five years you will love him as much as you do now?

ELIZABETH: Yes.

BESSIE: Do you think he will still love you as much then?

ELIZABETH: I hope so.

BESSIE: More?

ELIZABETH: More.

BESSIE: How about in fifty years—will you still love him then? If you're still alive. You could both be dead in fifty years. How old will you be when you've been married fifty years?

ELIZABETH: Seventy-four.

BESSIE: And Horace?

ELIZABETH: Seventy-seven.

BESSIE: You'll have gray hair then unless you dye it.

ELIZABETH: Yes. And my baby will be forty-nine.

BESSIE: And you'll have grandchildren and maybe even great-grandchildren. (ELIZABETH *cries.*) What's wrong?

ELIZABETH: I don't want to get old, Bessie, and I don't want Horace to get old. I want everything to stay as it is. When I'm seventy-two Mama and Papa will be dead unless they live to be a hundred. I don't want anybody I love to die, Bessie, ever, not Horace, not Mama, not Papa. Not Brother, not my sisters, not my baby I'm going to have.

BESSIE: What about me? Do you want me to die?

ELIZABETH: Oh, no. I don't want you ever to die.

BOBBY (*entering*): Excuse me, ladies, for not knocking. I forgot this room was rented. This used to be my room. I had a lovely time in Galveston, a little cold for bathing, but on sunny days we sat on the boardwalk and enjoyed the sunshine. My mother sends her regards. (HORACE *comes in.*) Hello, Horace.

HORACE: Hello, Bobby.

BOBBY: Did you hear about Mr. George Tyler? He took a butcher knife and stabbed himself through the heart. (*To* HORACE:) You were kin to Mr. George, weren't you?

HORACE: By marriage. Bessie, I passed your mother. She said if you were here to please come on home.

BESSIE: Yes Sir. (*She goes.*)

BOBBY: I want to show you good people a check I got today. (*He displays the check.*) It's for forty dollars. It's from Mr. Henry Vaughn, in payment . . .

HORACE (*interrupting*): We know about that, Bobby. We know all about that.

(Miss Ruth *sings* "*Lorena.*")

BOBBY: They say when she sang at the soldiers' benefit they announced her as the songbird of the South. (*He goes.*)

ELIZABETH: You didn't go to Miss Sarah's?

HORACE: No. I met Steve and the sheriff. Steve said there wasn't anything I could do. He said they have had Cousin Sarah under sedation ever since Mr. George ran away. He said she wouldn't see anybody. (*Pause.*) Sheriff said Mr. George wasn't quite dead when he got to him. He said he asked for me. He said he'd promised my daddy he'd look out for me.

MR. VAUGHN (*entering*): You heard about Mr. George?

ELIZABETH: Yes. It's terrible isn't it?

MR. VAUGHN: Yes, it is. Terrible. Terrible. Terrible. I brought some books over that I thought you should have, Horace. Some volumes of Wilkie Collins, Bulwer-Lytton and Thackeray. They belonged to your father, I believe. He had his name written in them. I got them years before from Senator Dockery. He said your father had given them to him in payment of a debt of some kind and after your father died he asked if I would like to buy them. He isn't a reader, he said. I bought the whole lot for twelve or fifteen dollars. I forget which now. I said to my wife the other night I think Horace should have them.

HORACE: Thank you.

MR. VAUGHN: Elizabeth says you think I don't like you.

ELIZABETH: Papa, I didn't say he told me that. I only said I felt he felt that way . . . Why . . .

MR. VAUGHN: Well, I do like you and respect you and . . . (*Pause.*) I hear you've been over to the bank to talk about a loan for opening a store.

HORACE: Yes Sir, but I won't need their help now. I can use the money I had been saving to buy a house.

MR. VAUGHN: I don't want you to spend all you've saved. Let me loan you the money to help you get started. And you can take whatever you've saved and buy Liberty Bonds. That way you'll be helping your country, too. Now, I have a lot of extra money right now. I have been very fortunate lately in a couple of land deals and I can let you have the money for your business. No interest at all. And you can pay me back whenever it's convenient and . . .

HORACE (*interrupting*): No Sir. Thank you. But I can't accept it. You've done enough for us already.

MR. VAUGHN: I want to help.

HORACE: Yes Sir. Thank you. But I couldn't let you.

MR. VAUGHN: Well, if you change your mind . . .

HORACE: Thank you.

MR. VAUGHN: Your mama didn't go shopping in Houston. She asked me to tell people that when they asked where she was, but I don't think she'd mind you knowing the truth. Actually she went to see about her sister, Lizzie. She's left her husband again and she doesn't have a dime, of course. Pride is fine if you can afford it, but she can't. She'll just have to go back to him and make the best of it, it seems to me. (*Pause.*) I think an unhappy marriage is the worst thing in the world. I'm happily married, thank God, and I trust you will be. Like I said to Mrs. Vaughn when Elizabeth asked about marrying you, I said . . . (*Pause.*) Well, that's all water over the dam isn't it? All water over the dam . . . Everyone says to me . . . Poor Horace . . . never had a father. Well, like I told Elizabeth, I never had a father either. (*Pause.*) And now I have no son. I'll hate myself for saying this tomorrow, but God forgive me I feel it; I have no son at all. He's a stranger to me. I don't know where to turn. (*Pause.*) There's peace in this room and contentment. That's why I like to come here, I think. I said to Mrs. Vaughn, "They don't have much but they're contented. You feel that." I hope you find contentment in your new home. I'd buy that for you, if I could, but of course, you know things like that can't be bought.

BOBBY (*entering*): Miss Ruth's in her room crying. I asked her what was wrong and she said her heart was broken.

ELIZABETH: Do you think I should go see about her?

HORACE: Oh, I don't know.

BOBBY: I explained to Miss Ruth that I was still married to a lovely girl in the sight of God.

MISS RUTH (*entering*): Oh, excuse me, I didn't know you had guests.

MR. VAUGHN: Come on in, Miss Ruth. I'm not staying long. Mrs. Vaughn is coming in on the Houston train.

MISS RUTH: It's too bad about Mr. George, isn't it?

ELIZABETH: Oh, yes.

MISS RUTH: I heard today about your new house and that you'll be leaving us soon. We'll miss Horace and Elizabeth, won't we, Mr. Bobby?

BOBBY: They had to elope to get married, you know. Elizabeth's mother and father . . .

ELIZABETH: That's all in the past now, Mr. Bobby. Everybody has forgiven everybody now. Papa is giving us this lovely new house. See?

BOBBY: That's nice to hear. I'm always happy when things turn out well. When did you all forgive each other?

ELIZABETH: Last Christmas.

MISS RUTH: In this very room.

BOBBY: Oh, yes. How long have you been married?

ELIZABETH: It will be a year this Valentine's Day.

BOBBY: And they're a very happy couple, you know. I remarked the other day to Mama, "I believe that's one marriage that will last." I remember the day Horace got married. It was Easter, Easter Sunday.

ELIZABETH: No, Mr. Bobby. It was Valentine's Day.

BOBBY: Do you all have a family plot reserved in the graveyard? I said to Mama the other night we don't have a family plot. We have to get one. I want us together even in death.

MR. VAUGHN: Miss Ruth, here's the house we're giving the children. We hope to have it ready in time for their new baby. Mr. Billy Lee was by my office this afternoon, Elizabeth. He was remembering the time he found you and Laura trying to find the graveyard to see Jenny's grave. He said he took the two of you out there and told you that she wasn't there, that she was in heaven. I'd forgotten that.

MISS RUTH: This is going to be lovely. I think I'm going to rent me a house of my own soon. I'm getting tired of trying to live in one room.

BOBBY: Mr. Billy Lee's oldest boy was a sissy.

MISS RUTH: He had a lovely singing voice though.

BOBBY: A very high tenor. He used to dress up in girl's clothes. Mr. Billy said he whipped the devil out of him everytime he caught him doing that, but he couldn't break him.

ELIZABETH: Jenny would have been twenty-three if she had lived.

MR. VAUGHN: Twenty-four. Her birthday was last week. Jenny was frail from the start. You were always healthy, Elizabeth. She was always sickly. Well, that's how it goes. One lives and one dies.

BOBBY: What ever became of Mr. Billy Lee's sissy boy? What was his name?

MISS RUTH: Edgar, he never married. I don't know where he is.

BOBBY: Oh, yes. The town was all excited last Valentine's Day. Every place you went all they talked about was Horace and Elizabeth eloping. It was all very romantic, you know. Bless their hearts, Mama said when I told her, bless their sweet hearts. It was a warm and lovely day, remember?

ELIZABETH: No, no, Mr. Bobby. It was raw and cold. I had picked a spring dress to marry in, low neck and it had no sleeves and I almost froze. I had to borrow a coat from Allie to keep warm.

BOBBY: Was it a large wedding?

ELIZABETH: No. Just Allie and Hector and the Baptist preacher and Horace.

MISS RUTH: And I was there. I sang, "Oh Promise Me" as they walked across the room to face the preacher.

ELIZABETH: Betty Norton, she was the flower girl, she carried a few roses we had gotten from Allie's yard. I began to cry in the middle of the ceremony and I think Horace thought I was sorry we were marrying.

BOBBY: Were you?

ELIZABETH: No.

BOBBY: Why were you crying?

ELIZABETH: I don't know. The next day was warm and

lovely though. I remember that the sun was shining and wedding presents began to arrive. Our first was a lovely cut glass pitcher from Horace's Aunt Virgie, and then . . . (*Pause.*) What was the next present, Horace, do you remember?

HORACE: No.

ELIZABETH: Oh, yes. A lovely hand-painted dish.

MR. VAUGHN: Who sent that?

ELIZABETH: Mr. George Tyler.

BOBBY: Edgar, Edgar Lee. Now what made me think of him? Oh, yes. We were talking about Mr. Billy Lee. (*There is silence.*) Mama saw Mr. Billy Lee whip Edgar once. She was over at Mrs. Lee's visiting one day and Mr. Billy came home and she said she heard him say, "Take that dress off," and then Edgar run across the yard in his sister's dress and Mr. Billy run after him and he grabbed him halfway across the yard and had his buggy whip and she said he beat him until she thought he would kill him. She said Mrs. Lee kept right on talking as if nothing had happened.

MR. VAUGHN: What kind of flowers did you say the Norton girl carried at your wedding?

ELIZABETH: Roses. I'd hoped to have sweetheart roses, but there were none growing in Allie's yard.

MISS RUTH: Have any of you heard when Mr. George Tyler's funeral will be?

HORACE: No, I'm sure it won't be for several days. He has relatives from all over the state and they'll want to give them time to get here.

MR. VAUGHN: Your mama planted sweetheart roses last fall next to Jenny's grave. She planted a red rose by Jenny's grave and a pink one by Daisy's.

BOBBY: Mama said Mr. Billy whipped Edgar until he bled. She said it was all she could do to sit there and watch.

ELIZABETH: I hope to have all kinds of roses in our yard after our house is built. Red roses, yellow roses, pink roses, sweetheart roses, and climbing roses.

(MISS RUTH *is singing "Oh Promise Me" quietly to herself as* ELIZABETH *joins in as the lights fade.*)

1918

Characters

HORACE ROBEDAUX
SAM GOLDMAN
ELIZABETH ROBEDAUX
BROTHER VAUGHN
BESSIE STILLMAN
MR. VAUGHN
MRS. VAUGHN
GLADYS MAUDE
IRMA SUE
DR. GREENE
MRS. BOONE
A BOY

Act One

Scene 1

Place: Harrison, Texas
Time: 1918

The lights come up downstage left on a graveyard plot. HORACE *is there looking at the grave sites.* SAM GOLDMAN, *carrying a hoe, comes over to him.*

SAM: What are you doin' out there this time of day, Mr. Horace?

HORACE: I'm having a tombstone put on my father's grave. Mr. Deitrick has ordered one for me, but I don't know which one is my father's . . . do you?

SAM: No. When was he buried?

HORACE: In 1902.

SAM: I don't know who worked here then. Wasn't there no marker on the grave?

HORACE: Must have been at one time. See there are three unmarked graves. My father is buried in one, my Uncle Cal and my Uncle Steve are buried in the others. I haven't been out here in a long time. My memory was that there was a board on each grave, but when Mr. Deitrick came out to look it over he said there were none.

111

SAM: Which one died first?

HORACE: My Uncle Steve.

SAM: Well, then, I think he would be the first grave.

HORACE: Beginning from which side?

SAM: That I don't know. Maybe some of the old-timers around could tell you.

HORACE: Maybe so.

SAM: There are a lot of graves out here. None of them marked. You have to get yourself a big, good tombstone if you wants your grave to stay marked. Even then you don't know, lots of the tombstones have fallen over and nobody has bothered to put 'em back up where they belongs. I don't do it, because I'm afraid I would put it back in the wrong place. The peoples that are buried in the vaults is the ones you're gonna always know where they're at. (*In the distance church bells ring.*) Isn't this flu terrible?

HORACE: Yes, it is.

SAM: Had three white funerals last week, all from the flu. Nobody I ever heard of though, all came from out in the country some place. Two colored funerals tomorrow. I just been over in the colored cemetery helping dig the graves.

HORACE: Who died?

SAM: Delia Washington, worked for Mrs. Moore.

HORACE: Sure. I knew her well.

SAM: She died this morning around five, and old George Harris.

HORACE: George Harris?

SAM: Yes Sir.

HORACE: My God! I ordered him a suit of clothes for Christmas. He just finished paying it out last week.

SAM: Then they're going to bury him in it.

HORACE: Did they both have the flu?

SAM: Yes Sir. Everybody's gettin' it. Black and white. Not sparin' anybody. I hear you're opening up a store.

HORACE: No, not for awhile now. I took the money I'd saved for that to buy war bonds last night at the rally. I figure there'll be plenty of time to open a store when the war's over.

SAM: You're gonna still have your cleaning and pressing shop?

HORACE: Oh, sure. And I have my line of tailor-made clothes.

SAM: I'm going to have to order me a new suit pretty soon. If I can afford it. High as everything is going. My God, everything is high!

HORACE: That's so. It's the war.

SAM: When's this war going to be over?

HORACE: I wish I knew.

SAM: We're winning . . . so they tell me . . .

HORACE: I hope so. Well, I don't know how to figure this, Sam. I have an uncle living out in East Texas. Maybe he'll remember. I guess I'll just have to write him. Mr. Deitrick will just have to hold the tombstone until I hear from him.

SAM: How come you bought your tombstone from Mr. Deitrick?

HORACE: I like him. He's always traded with me.

SAM: A lot of people won't have anything to do with him. They tell me because he's for Germany to win.

HORACE: I know that. I don't let him get started on the war with me. He knows how I feel.

SAM: Some folks say he should be locked up for the way he talks.

HORACE: I know. There are a lot of hotheads on both sides.

SAM: Are there other people around here want Germany to win?

HORACE: Sure there are.

SAM: What are they—Germans? They say Mr. Deitrick won't allow English to be talked in his house. You go in his house you got to talk German, or else. You ever been in his house?

HORACE: No.

SAM: I'd like to go. Just to hear him talk. They say he got his pictures of the Kaiser in every room and German flags flying everyplace. (*The church bells ring again.*) If I buy a suit, how much will I have to pay down?

HORACE: Whatever you can. Three dollars, five dollars. Then you pay it out so much a week.

(*A woman passes by. She is crying. She carries a small bouquet of flowers. SAM and HORACE watch her respectfully as she slowly walks past. They both take their hats off and nod solemnly to her. After she disappears offstage, SAM turns to HORACE.*)

SAM: Know who that is?

HORACE: No.

SAM: That's the widow of one of them country men that was buried the other day. I don't know which one. She comes here every day about this time with some flowers. You know Mrs. Stewart? She comes here every day rain or shine at four o'clock, summer and winter, and visits the grave of her boy that was drowned in the river. That's been four years now. Lots of ladies come out twice a week and visits their husbands' or their children's graves. Mrs. Goody, Mrs. Merriwether, Mrs. Bolton, Mrs. Jessie. After Mr. Willis and Mr. Hayhurst shot and kilt each other, both their widows would come out, sometimes be here at the same time, but they wouldn't speak. How old was you when your daddy died?

HORACE: Twelve.

SAM: I never knew my daddy at all. He died over at the prison farm before I was born.

HORACE: I wish you could help me out, Sam. But if you can't, I'll have to write my uncle and see what he can do.

SAM: How come you waited so long to put up a tombstone?

HORACE: I couldn't afford it before. (*He starts out.*) So long, Sam.

(*In the distance* MISS RUTH *sings "The Star Spangled Banner."*)

SAM: So long. Hope your uncle can tell you which one is which.

(*He goes off in one direction,* HORACE *in another, as the lights fade.*)

Scene 2

The lights come up downstage right on the living room of the recently built Robedaux house. The room is defined for us by its furnishings (it is not a particularly large room), an upright piano upstage right center, a dark oak dining room chair in front of the piano, a small partially upholstered couch, two large upholstered chairs. BROTHER VAUGHN *is by the piano looking at sheet music. In the distance* MISS RUTH *is singing "The Star Spangled Banner."*

BROTHER (*calling out to next room*): I wish Ruth Amos had stayed over by the river and never moved to this part of town. (*Calling louder:*) Sister . . .

(*From somewhere in the back of the house* ELIZABETH *answers.*)

ELIZABETH (*offstage*): What?

BROTHER: Did Ruth Amos sing at the war bond rally last night?

ELIZABETH (*offstage*): Yes.

BROTHER: What did she sing?

ELIZABETH (*offstage*): "The Star Spangled Banner." She forgot the words twice, poor thing. She gets very nervous when she sings in public.

BROTHER: I wish she'd forget the words now, or something. (*He sits at the piano, with one finger tapping out the melody of "Over There." A baby cries offstage. After a moment he calls:*) Sister, Sister. (*He goes to the edge of the room and calls even louder:*) Sister. Sister. Jenny is crying.

ELIZABETH (*offstage*): I hear her. Go pick her up will you, please? I'm feeding the chickens.

BROTHER: I'll feed the chickens. You get her.

ELIZABETH (*offstage*): All right. Thank you.

(BROTHER *starts out of the room when* BESSIE STILLMAN *comes silently into the room, and stands by the door.* BROTHER *turns and sees her.*)

BESSIE: Is Mary here?

BROTHER: Who?

BESSIE: Mary.

BROTHER (*calling*): Sister. That Stillman girl is here.

ELIZABETH (*offstage*): Who?

BROTHER: That Stillman girl, Bessie.

(*He goes out.* BESSIE *stands by the door for a beat and then quietly goes over to the piano and looks at the music. Then she peers mysteriously around the room.*)

ELIZABETH (*calling from offstage*): Hello, Bessie. Have a seat, Bessie. I'll be out in a minute.

BESSIE: Hello, Mary.

(BESSIE *goes to sofa and sits.* ELIZABETH *enters. She crosses to* BESSIE *and shows her the baby.*)

ELIZABETH: Look here. Hasn't she grown?

(BESSIE *looks down at the baby.* BROTHER *enters.*)

BROTHER: I fed the chickens.

ELIZABETH: Thank you. Bessie came to see me every day while we were living at the Pate house.

BROTHER: She calls you Mary.

ELIZABETH: I know she does.

BROTHER: Why does she call you that?

ELIZABETH: I don't know.

BROTHER (*to* BESSIE): Why do you call her Mary? (*She doesn't answer him. He turns to* ELIZABETH.) Doesn't she ever talk?

ELIZABETH: When she wants to. She used to be a big talker as a matter of fact.

BROTHER: Play some pieces, Sister.

ELIZABETH (*going to the piano and looking at the sheet music*): What would you like to hear?

BROTHER: "Over There." (*She begins to play and he sings the words. He gets halfway through. He stops.*) Sister, did Mama tell you I got kicked out of A & M?

ELIZABETH: Yes. (*She continues playing.*) I hope you'll not get discouraged and will go back next year.

BROTHER: I'm not going back. I want to go into the army. Papa said I could the day I turned eighteen. Papa was in a good humor this morning, let me tell you. You know how he is when he's in a good humor. Laughing and joking and hurrahing. I said, "Papa, you're in a good humor. I bet the price of cotton has gone up again." "No," he said. "What are you in such a good humor about then?" I said. "About Horace," Mama said. "Do you know Horace has saved four thousand dollars and pledged it all last night for war bonds?" (ELIZABETH *stops playing.*) Where did he ever get four thousand dollars, Sister?

ELIZABETH (*playing "I'm Always Chasing Rainbows"*): By working hard and saving. Was Papa really surprised?

BROTHER: I'll say. And happy.

ELIZABETH: That was the money he had saved to open a store of his own.

BROTHER: What about the cleaning and pressing shop?

ELIZABETH: He'll give that up when he has his store.

(HORACE *comes in. He goes over to* ELIZABETH *and kisses her.*)

HORACE: Hi, honey.

ELIZABETH: Did you decide which was your father's grave?

HORACE: I couldn't. I just have no way of being sure.

BROTHER: Wouldn't your mother know?

HORACE: No. She's never been near it. I have an Uncle Kyle in East Texas that might remember, and you know I bet Cousin Minnie would know. She has a keen memory.

BROTHER: How long ago was he buried?

HORACE: Sixteen years ago.

BROTHER: Wasn't there any kind of marker?

HORACE: Whatever there was is gone now. The family were all still so poor then they couldn't afford a permanent tombstone. No, I expect they put up wooden ones. I reckon a flood or a storm finally got them.

BROTHER: Sister says you're getting Mr. Deitrick to do it for you. He's a damn German spy. I heard Tucker May say he was going to form a posse and one night go over and burn his damn house down.

ELIZABETH: That's sounds like Tucker May.

BROTHER: Well, I think it's a disgrace the way he goes around saying he hopes the Germans will win and refusing to buy war bonds, and he has pictures of the Kaiser in every room of his damn house.

HORACE: Yes. I bet Cousin Minnie would know. I'll write her tonight. (*Pause.*) I told Mr. Deitrick plain to his face I did not believe in dual citizenship . . . whether Mexican, German or whatever. You can't be a citizen of two countries. If you live in America, you have to be an American; if you want to be a German, then you have to go to Germany.

BROTHER: Germany wanted Mexico to come in the war. Promised to give her Texas if she did when they won it.

HORACE: That would be the day.

BESSIE: Mary, I have to go now.

ELIZABETH: All right, Bessie. (*She takes the baby.* BESSIE *silently slips out of the house.*) Come back, Bessie.

HORACE (*going over to the baby*): Hello, honey. Excuse your daddy not speaking to you. I've been worried today.

ELIZABETH: What have you been worrying about? The war news is good.

HORACE: This tombstone business has about half driven me crazy.

ELIZABETH: You'll find someone to remember. Did you hear from your Aunt Virgie today?

HORACE: Yes, Willie came by the shop. She was on her way home from cooking some food for them. She says they're all about over it. Uncle Doc was still in and out of bed but Aunt Virgie was walking around. She says Aunt Inez's out of bed, but is still very sick. And Uncle T. still has fever.

BROTHER: Marshall Elmore and John Barclay are all sick, too.

HORACE: The porter from the Boone Hotel told me Clay has been out of his head for two days. He thinks he's in Germany fighting the Germans.

ELIZABETH: Allie called me this morning to say they got word from Milburn; he's in a hospital in France. He was badly gassed.

BROTHER: Leland Harris has been shellshocked. I wonder how that makes Lowell Murray and the other draft dodgers feel. I've got no respect for slackers. They can't even give loyalty to Germany for an excuse. They're just yellow-bellied cowards. I can't wait to get in there. If it's over before I can join up I don't know what I'll do.

HORACE: You can join anytime now you want to. They're takin' boys your age.

ELIZABETH: Papa made him promise he wouldn't join up until he was eighteen. (*Pause.*)

BROTHER: I wonder what it's like over there?

HORACE: Over where?

BROTHER: In Europe. I know it's not like here. I know that.

ELIZABETH: I'm sure not.

BROTHER: I wonder what it would be like to have people all around you that you can't understand. I've heard these names all my life—France, Belgium, Germany, Holland, Italy . . . (*Pause.*) Horace, don't you ever wonder what it would be like being there, or what it would be like when you got there? I wonder if it would look at all like Texas?

ELIZABETH: Well, Texas is certainly all different depending on where you are.

BROTHER: That's true.

ELIZABETH: And we have all different nationalities here.

HORACE: And a lot of them don't even bother to learn English.

BROTHER: If I tell you a secret, Horace, will you swear you won't let on I told you? (*Pause.*) Maybe I shouldn't tell you. Maybe I should wait and let Papa tell you.

HORACE: Tell me what?

BROTHER: I'm not going to tell you. I'll let Papa surprise you. (*Pause.*) Maybe I will tell you, but act surprised when you hear it again from Papa. You know what Papa is going to offer you? He was so impressed that you bought four thousand dollars' worth of war bonds that he told Mr. Thatcher, "I don't know why you're surprised. Horace is very patriotic."

MRS. VAUGHN (*offstage*): Lizzie . . .

ELIZABETH: We're in the living room, Mama.

(MR. *and* MRS. VAUGHN *enter.*).

MRS. VAUGHN: Marshall Elmore is at death's door, so is John Barclay.

ELIZABETH: We heard.

MRS. VAUGHN: The Cookenboos are all sick. I hope it hasn't started in our house. But we get everything, of course.

MR. VAUGHN: Horace, when I was going through the pledges last night after the rally and came across yours . . . one of the largest. You sure you meant four thousand dollars, not four hundred dollars, or forty dollars?

HORACE: No Sir. I meant that.

MRS. VAUGHN: Boy, you're not sick are you? You look so pale.

ELIZABETH: I think he's just tired. He went out to the cemetery to try to find out which of the unmarked graves in his family lot was his father's.

MR. VAUGHN: What do you want to know that for?

MRS. VAUGHN: He's putting a tombstone up for his father. I told you that. He's getting it from Mr. Deitrick.

BROTHER: Old Deitrick has pictures of the Kaiser in every room. Tucker May is going to organize a posse to burn his house down.

MRS. VAUGHN: That outlaw!

BROTHER: I think he should be called on. I think if he is going to live over here . . .

MR. VAUGHN (*sharply*): Be quiet, Brother. You don't know what you're talking about.

BROTHER: I'd like to see anyone say they were for Germany up at A & M. Why, we would have . . .

MR. VAUGHN (*snapping at him*): Well, you're not at A & M now. (*He sighs. He seems suddenly depressed.*) He flunked out. He didn't study.

BROTHER: How can I study when I have my mind on the war?

MR. VAUGHN (*angrily*): You have never studied. Not in grade school, not in high school.

MRS. VAUGHN: Now, Mr. Vaughn . . .

MR. VAUGHN: It's the truth. The God's pitiful truth. His record in school is a record of failure.

MRS. VAUGHN: Sh . . . now you were in such a good humor. Why spoil it all?

MR. VAUGHN: I'm not like Judge Haines. I want my children to all have educations. Maybe I do too much for them, maybe if they had to sacrifice to get an education, the way I did . . . they'd appreciate it more. After the war when I was growing up there was no one to do for you. We were lucky to have food on our table. I have gone to bed hungry, seen my mother, and brother and sisters hungry.

ELIZABETH (*hoping to change the subject*): Mama, did either of you remember going to Horace's father's funeral?

MRS. VAUGHN: I didn't go, did you, Mr. Vaughn?

MR. VAUGHN (*sulking*): I'm sure I did.

ELIZABETH: Would you remember where his grave was placed?

MR. VAUGHN (*leaving, obviously still depressed*): No. Let's go home, so they can have their supper.

MRS. VAUGHN: My goodness, Mr. Vaughn, have you forgotten why you came over here?

MR. VAUGHN (*curtly*): Oh, that's right. (*He takes out a red bandana handkerchief and blows his nose vigorously.*) I was talking to Mr. Thatcher in the office this morning. I was telling him of your buying four thousand dollars' worth of war bonds and he said he wasn't surprised . . .

BROTHER: Why isn't Robert in the army?

MR. VAUGHN: Because he's got flat feet.

BROTHER: I hear they paid a doctor to say so.

MRS. VAUGHN: Brother . . .

MR. VAUGHN: Shame on you spreading a story like that.

BROTHER: I'm only saying what I heard.

MR. VAUGHN: You're spreading stories about the son of a man of honor and my best friend.

BROTHER: I'm only saying what I heard. I heard it cost him . . .

MR. VAUGHN: Vicious lies . . . (*Thoroughly depressed:*) Let's go home.

MRS. VAUGHN: Mr. Vaughn, will you please tell Lizzie and Horace what you came to say?

MR. VAUGHN: Oh. (*Pause.*) Well, Mr. Thatcher said he wasn't surprised, that he knew you were very patriotic, that he was in front of Outlar's drug store the other morning and you were talking to some of your friends and he heard you say that if you didn't have the responsibility of a wife and child you would have been in France fighting from the day we declared war on Germany. And I've been thinking that over all day and this afternoon when I got home I told Mrs. Vaughn that none of us were doing enough for our country and that I was going to offer to take care of Elizabeth and the baby for the duration of the war so you could join and fight like you wanted to.

BROTHER: And Papa said I could join at the same time you did, didn't you, Papa?

MR. VAUGHN: Yes, I did. And I hope it straightens you out and gives you a little sense of responsibility. (*To* HORACE:) Well, that's my news. So you and Elizabeth talk it over.

HORACE: Well, that's very nice. Thank you, Sir. I do appreciate it.

MR. VAUGHN: I figure it's the least I can do for my country. You all talk it over now, and figure out when you can be ready to leave.

MRS. VAUGHN: If he wants to leave, Mr. Vaughn. Don't make up his mind for him. He and Lizzie should think seriously about it. It's serious, this whole war thing.

MR. VAUGHN: I know it's serious. I want them to talk it over. (*The phone rings.* HORACE *goes to answer it.*)

MRS. VAUGHN: What are you having for supper, Elizabeth?

ELIZABETH: Greens, pork roast, new potatoes, coleslaw.

MR. VAUGHN: What are we having?

MRS. VAUGHN: I don't know. I left it all up to Aunt Charity. I was working at the Red Cross all afternoon.

HORACE (*coming back in*): One of my colored customers died with the flu. He had a suit he was paying out on and his wife wanted to finish paying for it so he can be buried in it.

MR. VAUGHN: How much does he owe?

HORACE: I don't know exactly. I think about eighteen dollars. She only has ten. I said she can take the suit and pay me the rest a little at a time.

BROTHER: Syd Jackson is in the cavalry. I asked him how he got in there, and he said he asked for it. Would you like to be in the cavalry, Horace?

HORACE: I don't know. I hadn't thought about it.

MRS. VAUGHN: We'd better go and let you all have your supper.

MR. VAUGHN: You bought more war bonds than anybody last night. Did you know that?

HORACE: Yes Sir. I heard that.

MR. VAUGHN: Four thousand dollars. Elizabeth, did you know he was going to buy all these?

ELIZABETH: Yes Sir. We talked it over.

MR. VAUGHN: A man came up to me today and said your son-in-law must be rich buying four thousand dollars' worth of war bonds. "No," I told him, "he's not rich. Just patriotic."

MRS. VAUGHN: Mr. Vaughn said if we had more of Horace's kind of patriotism we'd have the war won in no time.

(MR. VAUGHN, MRS. VAUGHN *and* BROTHER *continue out of the room.*)

BROTHER: See you in France, Horace.

HORACE (*laughing*): Sure ... (*They leave.* HORACE *goes to* ELIZABETH. *He is obviously not at all overjoyed at* MR. VAUGHN'S *offer.*) What is your father talking about? I don't want to leave you and the baby. What in the world am I going to do, Lizzie?

ELIZABETH: Didn't you say that about going over to France?

HORACE: Maybe I did. I guess I was shooting off my mouth this morning in front of the drug store. The boys were ribbing me because I had you and the baby. They said I could talk patriotic because there was no danger I would ever have to go. But I never thought your papa would take it upon himself to make an offer like this.

ELIZABETH: Oh, why in the world does Papa always have to interfere? Well, you're just going to have to tell him you don't want to go.

HORACE: I guess. I hope he hasn't told about his offer all over town. I'll be the laughing stock if he has. I'll never hear the end of it.

ELIZABETH: Well, you'd better go over and tell him right now you don't want to go, or he will have it all over town.

HORACE: All right, but let me have supper first.

ELIZABETH: No. I wouldn't wait until after supper. I would tell him now.

HORACE: How am I going to tell him?

ELIZABETH: Just tell him.

HORACE: Do you think I should just walk in and say I don't want to go to France and leave Lizzie and the baby, or do you think I should say you and I appreciate a whole lot his generous offer, or anyway something like that, but in talking it over we have decided it is better to stay here until they start drafting married men.

MRS. VAUGHN (*re-entering*): Horace, I just heard T. Abell died from the flu.

HORACE: Oh, my God!

MRS. VAUGHN: No one called you?

HORACE: No.

MRS. VAUGHN: I thought maybe Virgie had called you.

HORACE: No one called me.

MRS. VAUGHN: You better go call her right away. (*He leaves.*) The whole town is coming down with it. Your papa says he isn't feeling at all well. John Barclay is very low, they say.

ELIZABETH: Does Papa have the flu?

MRS. VAUGHN: He thinks he does. I left a message for Dr. Greene to come over as soon as he can and examine him. I don't feel so well myself, to tell you the truth. But then, I don't dare get sick, all I have to do and tend to.

HORACE (*re-entering*): I talked to Uncle Doc. Aunt Virgie was over with Aunt Inez. Uncle Doc said he died half an hour ago. He was just going to call us. I said I'd be right over.

MRS. VAUGHN: I'd keep the baby here and let Lizzie go with you, but I don't think I should leave your papa, and if, God forbid, he has the flu, I don't think the baby should be around him.

HORACE: Does Mr. Vaughn have the flu?

MRS. VAUGHN: I'm not sure. But still he's not feeling well. I wouldn't care to take a chance.

ELIZABETH: Don't you want your supper before you go, Horace?

HORACE: No, I'll eat when I get back. (*He kisses her goodbye. He leaves.*)

MRS. VAUGHN: Your papa and I were talking about Horace, Elizabeth. You couldn't have a finer husband. I couldn't love him more if he were my own son. (*Pause.*) I wish Brother would turn out as well as he has. I told Mr. Vaughn whenever he gets too discouraged about him, look at Horace, how well he has turned out. He used to gamble and drink, he was raised on the streets practically, we never thought he'd amount to anything. We were in terror when you defied us and ran off and married him, and now look at him. He is a good husband, a good father, he doesn't drink or gamble any more, he has a business, he saved four thousand dollars just to buy war bonds and help the country out in this terrible war. (*Pause.*) Do you think he's going to take your papa's offer and enlist?

ELIZABETH (*uneasily*): I don't know.

MRS. VAUGHN: Milburn Hall is in a hospital in France. He has been gassed.

ELIZABETH: I know. Brother told me earlier.

MRS. VAUGHN: I'm glad Brother is old enough to go. It might just straighten him out.

ELIZABETH: I don't want Horace to go, Mama. (*Pause.*) He doesn't want to go, either. He was just on his way to tell Papa when you came over.

MRS. VAUGHN: Well, don't tell him now. Wait until he gets over whatever he has got. It will hurt his feelings so. He thought he was doing a wonderful, patriotic thing and you'd be so pleased. Both of you. (*Pause.*) To tell you the truth, I didn't think you would be at all. But you know how your papa is. He's always thinking of things for people he thinks they would like and then when they don't like it, or don't like it as much as he thinks they should like it, he gets his feelings hurt. (*Pause.*) Please don't ever say I said this, but his feelings were hurt when he gave you all the house and lot here and Horace insisted on keeping everything in your name.

ELIZABETH: I tried to explain to Papa why Horace did that. It had nothing to do with his not appreciating Papa's gift. He just didn't want anyone here to think that he was not standing on his own two feet. Horace felt since he was poor and had nothing . . . Oh, I really don't know how to explain it to you. It was pride, I guess, Mama.

MRS. VAUGHN: Don't bother to explain it to me. I didn't think anything about it. I'm just explaining how sensitive your father is. He thought Horace still held a grudge against him because he wouldn't speak to you after your marriage.

ELIZABETH: Horace has never felt any grudge.

MRS. VAUGHN: I know that. I'm just trying to explain how sensitive your father is, that's all. (*She looks over at the buggy. She goes to it and picks up the baby.*) The baby is growing so. She's such a good baby.

ELIZABETH: I'm thinking of hiring a nurse so I can start teaching piano again.

MRS. VAUGHN: I don't know where you'll find one. All the help I know are busy nursing people with the flu. Mrs. Cookenboo thinks the Germans brought the germs over here. She says it's part of what they call germ warfare. Well, I don't know how it got started, but I've never seen or heard of anything like it before in my life. Just take the families on this street that have come down with it: the Cookenboos, the Taylors, the Outlars, the Boltons. They're all down with it. The only families that haven't got it are the Wilsons and the Aldaghs. (*She puts the baby back in the carriage.*) I pray we'll all be spared or if we're taken it will be a mild case. Poor Inez. I wonder if T. left her anything? He was buying a farm from your papa out on the Burr Road, and I don't think it is even half paid for. T. was a young man still, thirty-six. It's the young ones the flu seems to get.

(ELIZABETH *rolls the baby carriage to another room.* MRS. VAUGHN *calls after her:*) They say Clay Boone is very low, too. Did I tell you that?

ELIZABETH (*calling back*): Someone told me—Brother, I believe. Or maybe it was Horace.

MRS. VAUGHN (*continuing to call out to her*): Mrs. Thatcher called me this morning and told me. She said they all dread anything happening to Clay. She said she thought Mrs. Boone would lose her mind if it did. She's so unstable, anyway.

BROTHER (*entering*): Mama, Papa says come on home, he needs you.

MRS. VAUGHN: Is he feeling any better?

BROTHER: No, worse.

ELIZABETH (*calling*): Who's that, Mama?

MRS. VAUGHN (*calling to her*): Your brother. He says your papa is feeling worse. He wants me to come home. (*To* BROTHER:) How do you feel?

BROTHER: All right. How do you feel?

MRS. VAUGHN: A little queasy, to tell you the truth.

ELIZABETH (*entering*): I have the baby in bed now.

MRS. VAUGHN: Does she sleep through the night?

ELIZABETH: Most nights.

BROTHER: Clay Boone died. They say you can hear Mrs. Boone screaming all over that end of town.

MRS. VAUGHN: Who told you?

BROTHER: Mrs. Thatcher called up. She said she was acting like a mad woman.

MRS. VAUGHN: Mercy! (*She starts out.*) Call me when Horace gets back and let me know how Inez is. (BROTHER *starts after her.*) Brother, you stay here with your sister until Horace comes home.

BROTHER: I'll stay for an hour. I have a date later on.

MRS. VAUGHN: Who with?

BROTHER: Delia.

MRS. VAUGHN: She won't be going out tonight, I hope. T. Abell is her uncle.

BROTHER: Oh, that's right. I hadn't thought about that.

MRS. VAUGHN: I bet she's over at Inez's right now. (*She leaves.*)

BROTHER: Sister, play some music.

ELIZABETH (*going to the piano*): What do you want me to play?

BROTHER: "I'm Forever Blowing Bubbles."

(*She begins to play it, gets halfway through a chorus and stops.*)

ELIZABETH: I don't feel like playing now. I wish Horace would come on back here.

BROTHER: You better get used to not having Horace around if he takes Papa's offer. If he goes over to France will you and the baby stay on here or move in with Papa and Mama?

ELIZABETH: I don't know.

BROTHER: We'd better hurry and join up or the war will be over.

ELIZABETH: I wish it were all over now.

BROTHER: Horace Wilson and Lou Owens leave tomorrow. They are going to camp in Georgia. (*Pause.*) Sister, I'm in trouble.

ELIZABETH: What kind of trouble?

BROTHER: Well . . . (*Pause.*) I don't know how to tell you.

ELIZABETH: Oh, my Father. (*Pause.*) Is it bad? (*Pause.*) Tell me that much.

BROTHER: It's pretty bad.

ELIZABETH: Oh, heavenly Father! Brother, please tell me what it is.

BROTHER: I got into a gambling game last night and I lost seventy-five dollars.

ELIZABETH: Who to?

BROTHER: Little Bobby Pate.

ELIZABETH: Brother!

BROTHER: I feel awful about it.

ELIZABETH: Why are you acting this way? Papa is gonna be furious.

BROTHER: I hope he never finds out.

ELIZABETH: He'll have to find out. Where will you ever in this world get seventy-five dollars?

BROTHER: I need more than that. That's only part of my trouble. I wish I was in the army right now. I wish I was in France. I wish I was dead. I wish . . .

ELIZABETH: Don't talk like that, Brother. Please don't talk that way.

BROTHER: I do. I do.

ELIZABETH: What have you done that's so terrible?

BROTHER: There was a letter just now waiting for me at home from a girl in College Station. She's having a baby. She wrote me she thought I was the father.

ELIZABETH: Are you?

BROTHER: I could be.

ELIZABETH: Are you going to marry her?

BROTHER: No. She don't want to marry me. She don't want to have the baby. She's going to get rid of the baby.

ELIZABETH: How?

BROTHER: I don't know. She wants me to send her a hundred dollars right away.

ELIZABETH: Oh, my God, Brother!

BROTHER: I can't help it.

ELIZABETH: Yes. You can.

BROTHER: How can I help it? Everybody in this damn family watching me all the time. Be like Papa. Be a fine, good, Christian man, like Papa. Well, I'll never be like him in a million years. I'm no damn good. (*Pause.*) Do you think Horace will loan me some money?

ELIZABETH: Horace? Horace don't have any money.

BROTHER: He had four thousand dollars for war bonds. He just bought a tombstone for his daddy's grave.

ELIZABETH: And that's *all* he has. Every penny. (*Pause.*) When did you find all this out?

BROTHER: Just now. Papa brought the letter when he came home.

ELIZABETH: You're going to have to tell Papa.

BROTHER: I can't.

ELIZABETH: Then I will.

BROTHER: You can't. Please . . . if you do I'll kill myself. Please . . . Please, promise me you'll never tell Papa or Mama. Promise me.

ELIZABETH: All right. (*Pause.*) I have two hundred dollars in my savings account that I saved when I taught piano. You can have it. (*Pause.*) But don't come back to me with your troubles. I'm sick and tired of them.

BROTHER: Thank you, Lizzie. I'll never forget this. Never. (*She gets her purse. She takes a check and writes it out.* BROTHER *looks at the paper.*) Who do you think has the greatest generals? Next to ours, of course. Everybody knows General Pershing is the greatest of them all. But I think the French come next. Don't you?

ELIZABETH (*giving him the check*): Here.

BROTHER: Thank you. I wonder what the battlefields of France are like. I saw Bobby Harron in this movie the other night. He was a doughboy, American, of course, and single-handed he defeated the whole German army. He started out a coward, see, but then he became brave and nothing could stop him. Not guns or cannons. I bet nothing will stop me when I get over there.

HORACE (*entering*): It's just pitiful. Aunt Inez and the two boys are sitting around stunned. T. had only been sick a week. A big strong man struck down like that. She said she'd have to turn the farm back to Mr. Vaughn, they were buying it from him. She said she could never afford to pay it out now. She doesn't know how she'll make a living for her boys. She has the two rent houses and cash enough to bury him and that's all. They're burying him day after tomorrow. They want me to be a pallbearer. (*Pause.*) Clay Boone is dead.

ELIZABETH: Brother told me.

HORACE: You can hear Mrs. Boone screaming all over that end of town.

ELIZABETH: Poor thing.

HORACE: Somebody said she was even cursing God for taking him away. (*Pause.*) Aunt Inez is pitiful. Her boys are pitiful. (*Pause.*) Walking back here through the cotton fields, crossing Old Caney I did a lot of thinking. I saw all of my mother's people, her sisters and brothers and their children that are left, that live here, crowding into the living room around Aunt Inez and her boys . . . and I thought of all that's come to each of them, and I was filled with dread. How can human beings stand all that comes to them? How can they? (*Pause.*) Your papa did let it out in town about his offer to me. Uncle Albert came up and spoke to me about it. He said it was a fine, patriotic thing your papa was doing, and he asked when was I leaving for the army. Not if I was going, but *when* I was going.

ELIZABETH: And what did you say?

HORACE: I said, "I'm leaving for the army the day after every able-bodied single man has volunteered or been drafted."

ELIZABETH: And what did he say?

HORACE: Nothing. He just got a sour look on his face. And then, I said I was afraid to go. I had a wife and a child I loved and I was afraid if I went I'd be killed and never see them again, and he said look at T. Abell. He might have been safer in the battlefields of France, anytime, than the pestilence here now.

BROTHER: You're not going to accept Papa's offer, Horace?

HORACE: No.

ELIZABETH: But don't tell Papa until he's feeling better. I promised Mama we wouldn't.

BROTHER: I hope Papa will still let me join up. (*Pause.*) Are you really afraid to go, Horace?

HORACE: Yes, and I just decided I was going to admit it.

BROTHER: What if they start drafting married men?

HORACE: Then I'll have to get over being afraid. John Barclay died twenty minutes after Clay Boone.

ELIZABETH: Oh, my God!

BROTHER: Maybe your uncle is right. Maybe we'd all be better off in France. I know the Germans sent these germs over here, that's the only way they have left to lick us. They're barbarians. They'll stop at nothing. The dirty Huns. I'll see you in the morning. (*He leaves.*)

HORACE: I don't feel so hot myself. I ache all over. (*He laughs.*) I've heard so much about the symptoms of the flu I don't know whether I'm getting it, or whether I'm imagining it.

ELIZABETH: Can I get your supper for you now?

HORACE: No thank you.

ELIZABETH: You should have something to eat.

HORACE: I'm not hungry. (*Pause.*) Walking through the fields, through Old Caney, I thought how is it possible on this beautiful night men are dying? Here or in Europe, or anywhere. And I thought, Death, if I don't think of you, you'll vanish. I'll think of life. My life with Lizzie and the baby. All the happiness and goodness that have come to me since you married me. (*He feels his forehead.*) Feel my head, Lizzie. (*She does so.*)

ELIZABETH: You have a fever. You better get to bed. (*He starts away.*) Honey, where are you going?

HORACE: To find a pen and paper. I have to write Uncle Kyle and Minnie about Papa's grave. Mr. Deitrick is waiting to know where to place the tombstone. (*He begins to search for paper and pen.* ELIZABETH *goes to stop him, when there is a knock on the door. She goes.* IRMA SUE *is there.*)

ELIZABETH: Come in, Irma Sue. (*She comes into the room.*)

IRMA SUE: Hello, Mr. Horace.

HORACE: Good evening. (*He continues his search for writing materials.*) I can't find paper and pen, Elizabeth.

ELIZABETH: Look in the bedroom. (*He goes.*)

IRMA SUE: Miss Elizabeth, Mama just heard you are thinking about giving piano lessons again.

ELIZABETH: Yes, I'm hoping to.

IRMA SUE: Mama said to ask you if you do teach, can Sister and me study with you?

ELIZABETH: Yes, you can.

IRMA SUE: Where did you study music?

ELIZABETH: Kidd Key.

(HORACE *comes out with pen and paper.*)

IRMA SUE: Hello again, Mr. Horace.

HORACE: Hello. (*He starts to write, half talking to himself as he does so.*) Some of the family think Minnie is very sensitive and peculiar, but she was always good to me.

ELIZABETH: Mr. Horace isn't feeling well, honey. I think you'd better go home now. You come back and visit when he's feeling better.

IRMA SUE: You got the flu, Mr. Horace?

ELIZABETH: We don't know that.

IRMA SUE: I had the flu, all of us did, but it was a mild case. We have it all behind us now.

HORACE (*still half to himself*): When I saved the money to go to business school in Houston, I was lost at first, because I had only gone to the sixth grade here and I thought I just would have to give up and come back here, because I couldn't seem to understand anything they were talking about.

ELIZABETH: Do me a favor, Irma Sue, honey. Run over to Papa's through our back yard and see if Dr. Greene is still there, and if he is have him come over here as quick as he can.

IRMA SUE: Yes Ma'am. (*She runs out.* ELIZABETH *goes to the door to watch.*)

HORACE (*talking to himself throughout all this*): But Minnie was living in Houston then and she wouldn't hear of my leaving. She had gotten a college degree, some way, and was a schoolteacher in Houston, and every afternoon, when she finished teaching, and every night she would coach me. (ELIZABETH *goes to him. She feels his forehead.*) I'm trying to write a letter, Lizzie, but I can't think. I feel very dizzy. Everything looks so peculiar. Where is Mama?

ELIZABETH: Now, she's in Houston. You know where she is.

HORACE: She's married to Mr. Davenport.

ELIZABETH: Yes. (HORACE *sways as he tries to get up.*) Now just sit here. Dr. Greene has been sent for.

HORACE: Dr. Greene? Who is Dr. Greene?

ELIZABETH: Now you know who he is, honey.

HORACE: I always preferred Dr. Andrews.

ELIZABETH: Now, sh, you musn't say that. If Dr. Greene heard you say that it would hurt his feelings.

HORACE: Where is Dr. Andrews?

ELIZABETH: He's dead.

HORACE: When did he die?

ELIZABETH: Oh, a number of years ago.

HORACE: Do I have a fever?

ELIZABETH: I think so.

HORACE: Call Mama in Houston and tell her I have a fever, but tell her not to worry, I'll be all right in the morning.

ELIZABETH: I will.

HORACE: Call her now.

ELIZABETH: In a little.

HORACE: After my mother married Mr. Davenport she never felt free to have me in her house. While I was living in Houston I was supposed to have breakfast with her every morning, and one morning I came over to get my breakfast and she met me at the door and there was terror in her eyes and I heard her say, "Well, thank you for buying me the eggs and milk. I'll see you later," and I knew something was wrong and then I saw Mr. Davenport back in the kitchen and I knew he had not gone to work that day for some reason, and that she didn't dare have him know that she was giving me breakfast, or helping me in any way . . .

(DR. GREENE *comes into the room.*)

ELIZABETH: I'm glad to see you, Doctor.

DR. GREENE (*going to* HORACE): Hello, Horace.

HORACE: Mr. Davenport gave Sister everything she wanted, a piano, piano lessons, but he would not allow Mama to help me in any way.

DR. GREENE: That's all right now. You're going to be fine.

HORACE: He'd had to work from the time he was twelve and had no help from anyone, so that's what he thought a boy should do. But I never felt comfortable or welcome in my mother's house from the day she married him.

DR. GREENE (*getting a stethoscope and thermometer from his doctor's bag*): Your papa has come down with the flu. Your mama said that's why she didn't come over with me.

HORACE: Sh . . . Sh . . . Can you hear them? There's Marshall and Willis and . . . there's General Pershing and

Mr. Vaughn. Mr. Vaughn is the General now. He pinned my medal on me. "Over there . . . Over there . . ." Get me my uniform, honey. God help me, I'm afraid. I'm afraid . . . Where is Lizzie? I've lost Lizzie and my little girl in France.

ELIZABETH: You haven't lost anybody, honey. We're here. (*She holds him.*) Sh . . . Sh . . . now. Dr. Greene can't take your temperature unless you're quiet. (HORACE *rests against her.*)

DR. GREENE: Open your mouth, Horace. (*He does so. The doctor puts the thermometer inside.*) Now keep quiet for a few minutes.

(DR. GREENE *looks at his watch.* HORACE *looks up at* ELIZABETH.)

ELIZABETH: Sh . . . Sh . . .

(DR. GREENE *takes the thermometer out of* HORACE'S *mouth. He looks at it. He goes over to his bag.*)

HORACE: Do you love me, Elizabeth?

ELIZABETH: I love you.

HORACE: Don't let me die, Elizabeth.

ELIZABETH: You are not going to die.

HORACE: Hold me.

ELIZABETH: I'm holding you.

(HORACE *faints.*)

Dr. Greene . . .

DR. GREENE (*coming over to them*): He's very sick, Elizabeth. You'll need some help. (*He gets smelling salts out of his case. He revives* HORACE.)

HORACE: What happened?

DR. GREENE: Nothing. It's all right now. (*He closes his bag. He starts away.* ELIZABETH *follows him.*)

ELIZABETH: Will you call Mama and tell her?

DR. GREENE: Your mama can't help you. She's busy nursing your papa.

ELIZABETH: Oh, that's right.

DR. GREENE: I'll try and get some kind of help over here for you.

ELIZABETH (*whispering*): Is Papa very sick?

DR. GREENE (*whispering*): I don't think so. Not as sick as Horace.

ELIZABETH (*whispering*): Horace is very sick?

DR. GREENE (*whispering*): He's very sick. Get him to bed right away. I'll leave this medicine for you. I'll have more in the morning. (*He gets his bag. He starts away.*) And I'd keep him away from your baby if I were you.

ELIZABETH: Yes Sir.

(*He goes.* ELIZABETH *returns to* HORACE.)

HORACE: Lizzie, sing to me.

ELIZABETH: Sh . . . Sh . . .

HORACE: Please, sing to me.

ELIZABETH: All right. What do you want me to sing?

HORACE: "It's a Long Way to Tipperary." (ELIZABETH *sings. He joins in.*) Don't let me die.

ELIZABETH: You're not going to die. (*She continues singing, holding him.*)

Act Two

Scene 1

The lights come up on upstage right on a bedroom in the Robedaux house, a few weeks later. HORACE *is in bed.*

ELIZABETH *is there in her gown and robe. She has a bowl of soup and a spoon. She sits by* HORACE's *bed watching him. After a moment she quietly gets up and tiptoes out of the room into the living room. She sits down and picks up a hymnal. She finds a hymn, "I Look to Thee in Every Need," and begins to sing it quietly to herself.*

HORACE (*calling weakly*): Elizabeth . . .

(*She stops singing and comes back into the bedroom.*)

ELIZABETH: Did you wake up again? Are you still hungry? I can heat the soup up. There's half a bowl left.

HORACE: I'm not hungry.

ELIZABETH: Try to get back to sleep now.

HORACE: I'm not sleepy. (*Pause.*) Where am I?

ELIZABETH: You're home in bed. Sh . . . Don't talk now, you still need to save your strength. You're ever so much better, but Dr. Greene says . . .

HORACE (*weakly, interrupting*): Elizabeth . . .

ELIZABETH: There's really nothing to worry about now, the doctor says. It's all behind you now.

HORACE: What is?

ELIZABETH: The flu.

HORACE: Did I have the flu?

ELIZABETH: Yes. Don't you remember?

HORACE: I remember something about it. But I thought I had gotten well and then you and the baby got sick.

ELIZABETH: That's right. You had it and then you got better and I took it and the baby took it, and you were waiting on us, and then you just keeled over, fainted right on the floor. I was so scared. The doctor said you had gotten up too soon and tried to do before you should and had a relapse, and this time you were so sick; I couldn't get out of bed to wait on you, because I was still sick, Brother came over then—he never did get it—and he called Aunt Virgie, as Mama and Papa were both in bed still then, and Aunt Virgie came over and nursed us until I got my strength back.

HORACE: Where is Auntie now?

ELIZABETH: She went home yesterday. Don't you remember? The doctor said you were out of danger now and she told you goodbye and . . . (*He begins to cry.*) Horace, don't. Please don't cry. It's all over now. Terrible as it was, it's all behind us now.

HORACE: I thought I was going to die. I remember now. I thought I was dying, and I was going to leave you forever and I wanted so badly to live.

(MRS. VAUGHN *and* BROTHER *come into the bedroom.*)

MRS. VAUGHN: Well, how's the patient?

ELIZABETH: He's pretty well today. He's still pretty weak . . .

MRS. VAUGHN: I made some custard especially for you, Horace. It's very nourishing. I put it in the kitchen, Elizabeth.

ELIZABETH: Thank you.

MRS. VAUGHN: I'd also fix him a little grits, with lots of butter. That will help get his strength back.

MR. VAUGHN (*tentatively entering the bedroom*): Hello, Horace.

HORACE: Hello, Mr. Vaughn.

MR. VAUGHN: We thought we had lost you, son. We just about gave you up last week. Brother came running over last Friday and he said if you want to see Horace alive again, you'd better hurry and get over there. Weak as the flu had left Mama and me, we dressed and came running over. I stood right here by you and you opened your eyes and you said, "Mr. Vaughn, do you know what I want to do?" "No, son," I said, "what?" "I want to live." "I want you to live too, Horace." "Yes Sir, but I want my life to be spared so I can join the army and serve my country."

HORACE: Did I?

ELIZABETH: He was delirious, Papa. He didn't know what he was saying.

MRS. VAUGHN: Clay Boone was delirious like that just before he died and they say he thought he was in France fighting the Germans.

BROTHER: Howard Cunningham tried to stab his own mother with a butcher knife; he thought she was a German. Of course, he was so weak he couldn't have done any harm. I don't think any of them knew where they were, or what they were saying, no more than if they were drunk or . . .

MR. VAUGHN (*interrupting*): Horace knew what he was saying. I think he knew exactly what he was saying. Didn't you, son?

BROTHER: Shoot, he didn't know what he was sayin' no more than the others did.

MR. VAUGHN: How do you know so much about it? What makes you so much of an authority?

BROTHER: I heard Dr. Greene say so. He said none of them knew what they were doing or talking about. One night Horace thought he was at a dance at the Opera House, and he was upset because you had told Sister she wasn't allowed to dance, and he said . . .

MR. VAUGHN: I don't want to hear what he said. (*Pause.*) I still think that's why his life was spared by the Lord. He had this higher purpose waiting for Horace.

BROTHER: I didn't get the flu at all, Horace. The day they thought you were going to die, fifteen others died here. They had prayer meetings in all the churches praying for our deliverance.

HORACE: Anybody die that I knew?

BROTHER: A lot. Howard Cunningham, Marshall Elmore, Max Rosebury. Hardin Estell, Mae Davis . . .

MRS. VAUGHN: She left four motherless children.

MR. VAUGHN: Now do you see why I think you have been spared for a special purpose?

HORACE: How is the war going?

BROTHER: We're winning. No doubt about that. It won't be long before it's over. I'm going next month . . . Papa said I could . . .

MR. VAUGHN: You better hurry and get your strength back, Horace, if you want to get over there before it's all over.

BROTHER: Fred Rowan was killed in France last week.

MRS. VAUGHN: He left three small children. Isn't that pitiful?

BROTHER: Tucker May killed Steve Aldridge. He shot him over a boundary dispute. Steve moved a fence on land Tucker said was his, so Tucker got his gun and killed him.

MRS. VAUGHN: Steve left seven children. His wife is very bitter.

ELIZABETH: What are they going to do to Tucker? Nothing as usual?

BROTHER: They're all scared of him. The sheriff and all his deputies. He said it was self-defense.

ELIZABETH: They ought to send him over to France, he likes to fight so much.

BROTHER: How many men has Tucker killed, Papa?

MR. VAUGHN: I don't know.

MRS. VAUGHN: They ought to send him over and Teddy Hopkins and Banks Dickey and all the other bullies in this town. Maybe they'd get some of the fighting out of their systems.

BROTHER: Mrs. Murray slapped Mrs. Oliver's face at the bridge party the other day because she implied Dorian was a slacker.

MR. VAUGHN: Well, isn't he? He's not in the army. He's twenty-two. (BROTHER *whistles "Over There."*) Maybe you and Brother could join up at the same time, Horace. I asked him to wait awhile longer to join until you had a chance to get your strength back.

ELIZABETH: Papa, I think Horace is tired. I think we'd all better go into the other room and talk. Don't you feel like sleeping, Horace?

(*They all start out of the room.*)

HORACE: Elizabeth . . . (ELIZABETH *comes back into the room. The others continue off into the kitchen.*) Elizabeth, I hate to ask you this. You're gonna think for sure the flu has left me half crazy. But I keep thinking . . . I know it is just the fever . . . like my saying to Mr. Vaughn I wanted to live to join the army. Now you know I was out of my mind then . . . the baby . . . Elizabeth, I kept dreaming you told me she was dead. (*She cries.*) Oh, honey, my dreams shouldn't get you upset. They shouldn't. It was the fever. I know I must have had a very high temperature. I dreamed all kinds of crazy things.

ELIZABETH: It wasn't a dream, Horace. She died a week ago.

HORACE: Oh, my God! (*He turns away from* ELIZABETH.) Was there a funeral?

ELIZABETH: Yes. I told you at the time. Don't you remember any of it? (*He shakes his head "no."*) We couldn't go, either of us. (*She cries.*) She died, and I couldn't nurse her or see to her. Mama had to get Aunt Charity to come over and nurse her for us, until she got sick with the flu and then . . . (*Pause.*) Your aunt came back. She was rocking her in her arms when she died. (HORACE *turns his head away from her.*) I was half crazy. I couldn't think. We didn't know whether to tell you, sick as you were, but finally, I felt I had to tell you and you listened to me as if you understood it all. I had her buried in your family's plot instead of Papa's. I think that hurt Mama and Papa but I wanted to do what I thought you'd want and we didn't have our own family lot.

(*In the distance bells are ringing. A siren sounds.* BROTHER *comes running in.*)

BROTHER: Armistice! Armistice! Armistice has been declared!

ELIZABETH: Oh, no.

BROTHER: That's why they're ringing the bells. (*Bells continue to ring.* BROTHER *gives a whoop.*) Germany has surrendered. We've licked the Kaiser.

MRS. VAUGHN (*running in*): Isn't it wonderful? (*She cries.*) Thank God. Thank God it's all over. Your papa called the newspaper and they've had a wire confirming it. He's calling the Thatchers and the Cookenboos now to tell them. They'll be so happy. Lee and Buster are still in training camp in San Antonio. Mrs. Cookenboo said the other day she had this feeling they would never go overseas and she was right.

BROTHER: I'm going uptown. There'll be lots of excitement in town, I bet. (*He goes running out.*)

(MRS. VAUGHN *looks at* ELIZABETH *and* HORACE. *They're silent and withdrawn.*)

MRS. VAUGHN: What's the matter? Oh, I know. I know. I'm sorry, forgive me.

ELIZABETH: Horace didn't remember about the baby. He thought he had dreamed it. He thought . . . (HORACE *is crying again.*) Don't cry, honey. It's not good for you. You're still weak. (*They both are crying now.*) Mama, help us. How did you stand it when you lost your children?

MRS. VAUGHN: You just stand it. You keep going.

ELIZABETH: Of course, you had other children.

MRS. VAUGHN: I had only you when I lost the first little girl, but when I lost the second, I had four others then. There were times when you were growing up I despaired for each of you.

ELIZABETH: We had the baby buried right next to your father's grave. I had Mama order a tombstone like the one she has on my little sister's grave. I thought I'd like a lamb on it like they have on theirs. (*Pause. In the distance a band plays.*) I slipped out there yesterday afternoon and visited her grave. I took some flowers from our yard. (*She cries.*)

MRS. VAUGHN: She's at peace, honey. She's at peace. (*Pause.*) When we lost our second child your papa was sitting in the living room by her little coffin. Mrs. Coon Ferguson came into the room and said, "Mr. Vaughn, did you ever think the death of this child was a judgement on you for not joining the church?" And his face flushed crimson, but he just said very quietly, "No, Mrs. Ferguson, I never did."

HORACE: You say you buried her next to my papa?

ELIZABETH: Yes.

HORACE: How do you know where Papa's buried?

ELIZABETH: We got a letter from your Cousin Minnie. She remembers. She wanted to come out and show you, but I asked her not to.

HORACE: Cousin Minnie always said there were two sides to the story of Papa and Mama. She said I had only been told Mama's side.

MRS. VAUGHN: Your mama was a fine woman, son. She did all she could do. Your father was a fine man, bright, educated. But he had the responsibility of that whole family. They had been so rich and then when they lost their shipping fleet during the war . . . and they came here penniless . . . they all looked to your father to do for them. Your Uncle Robedaux just sat around reading Greek. Your mother had two small children and they all moved in with her. Your grandmother, two boys, your Aunt Sally, three grandchildren.

ELIZABETH: Your mama and sister wrote a sweet letter when they heard about the baby . . .

BESSIE (*calling at the living room door*): Mary . . . Mary . . .

ELIZABETH (*going to answer*): Hello, Bessie. I can't ask you in, Bessie. Horace is still sick. (BESSIE *stands looking at her.*) Did you hear what happened to Jenny? (BESSIE *shakes her head.*) Have you been sick, too, with the flu, honey? (BESSIE *nods her head "yes."*) Your mother didn't tell you what happened to Jenny? (*She shakes her head "no."*) Jenny died, honey. She had the flu, too, and she died. (BESSIE *stands staring at her.*) Now, you run on, honey. And come back another day and visit me.

(BESSIE *leaves.* ELIZABETH *follows her outside the area. She stands watching as* BESSIE *goes off. She continues standing there during the next scene.*)

(HORACE *has closed his eyes.* MRS. VAUGHN *looks over at him. She tiptoes out of the room into the living room.* MR. VAUGHN *comes hurrying into the living room area.*)

MR. VAUGHN: Come on. I want you to come with me to the Courthouse. Everyone in town is going. They're going to have a big rally to celebrate the end of the war.

MRS. VAUGHN: I don't feel like going. I don't feel like celebrating anything with little Jenny dead, and anyway I don't think I should leave Elizabeth alone here with Horace. She still hasn't her strength back. I'm going to fix supper for them. (*Pause.*) Elizabeth told me this morning she's expecting another baby.

MR. VAUGHN: When?

MRS. VAUGHN: In another six months or so. She isn't exactly sure. The doctor says he'll be able to tell better next month. She hasn't told Horace yet, so don't let on I've told you anything.

MR. VAUGHN: I won't. (*Pause.*) I have to speak to her about that business about Brother.

MRS. VAUGHN: Well, don't bother her now with that.

MR. VAUGHN: She knows about it already. She loaned him two hundred dollars to pay Bobby Pate and that girl.

MRS. VAUGHN: Tell her some other time. Not tonight.

MR. VAUGHN: Maybe you'll tell her. Here's a check for her.

MRS. VAUGHN: All right. But I don't want to tell her either, tonight. Horace hadn't remembered about Jenny's death.

MR. VAUGHN: He hadn't?

MRS. VAUGHN: No.

MR. VAUGHN: They got word today Lawton Davis was killed two months ago in France.

MRS. VAUGHN: Why did it take so long for them to notify them?

MR. VAUGHN: They had a hard time identifying the body some way. (*A band plays a medley of World War I and Southern favorites.*) His mother called you just before I left. I told her to call you over here; she said she didn't want to bother you here. She said she wanted your advice about whether they should bring his body here for burial or leave it over there.

MRS. VAUGHN: Can they bring it here?

MR. VAUGHN: I guess so. From what she said.

MRS. VAUGHN: I wouldn't know how to advise about that, Mr. Vaughn. Would you?

MR. VAUGHN: No. I wouldn't. (*Pause.*) What am I going to do about Brother, Mrs. Vaughn? I'm at my wit's end. What's to become of him?

MRS. VAUGHN: He'll find himself. He's just climbing fool's hill.

MR. VAUGHN: I don't know. I hope so . . . but look at my brother. Dissipation ruined his life. Dead at forty-two. Two wives. Never anything but trouble to all of us. (*Pause.*) A friend of mine has some cotton boats sailing between Galveston and New York. He said he would give Brother a job working on one of his boats. I think I'm going to tell him he has to go. It will be hard work, which will be good for him and it will keep him away from these trifling friends of his here.

MRS. VAUGHN: Whatever you say.

(*Pause.*)

MR. VAUGHN: Maybe I shouldn't go to the Courthouse either. I promised to make a speech but someone else can do it for me.

MRS. VAUGHN: No. You go on. You should be there. After all you were head of the war bond loans . . . and on the draft board. Would you like some supper before you go?

MR. VAUGHN: No; I'll get some oysters downtown.

(*He leaves.* MRS. VAUGHN *goes outside.* ELIZABETH *is still in the yard. She is listening to the music from the band.* MRS. VAUGHN *and* ELIZABETH *embrace.*)

MRS. VAUGHN: They're having a victory celebration at the Courthouse. Your papa is going to make a speech.

ELIZABETH: Are you going?

MRS. VAUGHN: No, I don't feel like going. I thought I'd fix us some supper whenever you are hungry.

ELIZABETH: Thank you.

MRS. VAUGHN: Are you hungry now?

ELIZABETH: No.

MRS. VAUGHN: You're not eating. You must eat.

ELIZABETH: I've no appetite. I have to call Mr. Deitrick tonight, and Horace's Cousin Minnie wrote asking him if he would also have tombstones put on his father's brothers' graves. She said she will pay for them. I don't want to bother Horace with it. Is he sleeping?

MRS. VAUGHN: Yes.

ELIZABETH: He's so thin. He seems to have lost so much weight.

(*Band music plays again. Fireworks go off in the distance. Horns and sirens sound from time to time.*)

MRS. VAUGHN: It is quite a celebration. (*Pause.*) When are you telling Horace about the new baby?

ELIZABETH: I'll tell him tonight or tomorrow.

MRS. VAUGHN: He'll be pleased, I know.

(*She puts her arm around* ELIZABETH. ELIZABETH *kisses her on the cheek and goes into the house. She looks into* HORACE's *bedroom. He is awake. He calls to her.*)

HORACE: Elizabeth . . . (*She goes into the room.*) The war's over, isn't it?

ELIZABETH: Yes. That band is at the Courthouse. Everyone is down there celebrating.

HORACE: I'm not sure any more of what I've been told and haven't been told.

ELIZABETH: Your memory will be as good as new in a day or so. (*Pause.*) I'm going to have a baby, Horace.

HORACE: When?

ELIZABETH: In about six months. Dr. Greene can't be too sure.

HORACE: Well . . . that's something.

ELIZABETH: Are you pleased?

HORACE: I sure am. Are you pleased?

ELIZABETH: Yes.

(*Pause.*)

HORACE (*closing his eyes*): I'm still so weak, Lizzie. Do you think I'll ever get my strength back?

ELIZABETH: Of course, you will. It all takes time, Dr. Greene says. You have to be patient.

HORACE: How long has the shop been closed?

ELIZABETH: Almost a month.

(*Band music plays again.*)

HORACE: What's the date today?

ELIZABETH: November 11th.

HORACE: And the war is over?

ELIZABETH: Yes.

(HORACE *sings half to himself, "Over There . . . Over There."*)

HORACE: I keep forgetting about Jenny. I keep waiting to ask where is she. You said you ordered her tombstone?

ELIZABETH: Yes.

HORACE: And you know for sure which grave is my father's?

ELIZABETH: Yes.

HORACE: I don't suppose Mr. Deitrick has gotten his tombstone up?

ELIZABETH: Yes. He has. It was there when I visited Jenny's grave yesterday. Minnie wrote and asked that I have tombstones placed on the graves of your father's brothers. She said she would pay for them. I'll call Mr. Deitrick tonight.

HORACE: Did she know about Jenny's death?

ELIZABETH: Yes. She said she was heartbroken for us.

HORACE: She never got to see her.

ELIZABETH: No.

HORACE: A lot of people never got to see her. My mother never did, my sister. I'm glad we had her christened without waiting for Mama to get out. Hand me Jenny's picture, honey.

(*In the distance band music plays.* ELIZABETH *gets the picture and gives it to* HORACE. *He looks at it for a beat. He puts it down. He whistles "Over There" softly to himself.*)

DR. GREENE (*entering*): How's Horace?

MRS. VAUGHN: He's much better. Shall I tell him you're here, Dr. Greene?

DR. GREENE: No. I was just passing by and I thought I'd inquire.

MRS. VAUGHN: Are you able to get some rest now?

DR. GREENE: A little.

MRS. VAUGHN: It's wonderful about the war being over.

DR. GREENE: Yes. (*Music plays.*) Why aren't you at the celebration?

(*She points toward the house.* HORACE *is asleep.* ELIZABETH *leaves.*)

How is Elizabeth?

MRS. VAUGHN: You know Elizabeth. She is like a pine knot. She says she's going to start teaching piano again. Do you think she's strong enough to do that?

DR. GREENE: I think so.

(BESSIE *comes in.*)

MRS. VAUGHN: Hello, Bessie. Did you have the flu? (*No answer.*) Did any of your family have the flu?

(*In the distance* MISS RUTH *sings "Peace Be to this Congregation."*)

I know what Ruth Amos' solo is going to be this Sunday. That's her favorite. Everytime it's her turn to sing a solo she picks that one. I wish she'd get a new favorite.

BESSIE: Is Mary home?

MRS. VAUGHN: Yes, honey. But she can't see you. She won't be able to see anybody for awhile. You run on now. When she gets well enough to see you we'll get word to you. (BESSIE *leaves.*) She calls Elizabeth Mary. I don't know why she does that. My name is Mary. I don't think any of her family had the flu.

DR. GREENE: I don't remember hearing one way or the other. I'm not their doctor.

MRS. VAUGHN: If they had it, they were over it by the time the baby died. They sent flowers to the funeral. One of the few families in town that did. Everybody was so busy thinking about their own dead they didn't have time to worry with anyone else's grief. (*Pause.*) It's so quiet isn't it? War and death seem so far away. So very far away.

DR. GREENE: It was cold this morning, Mrs. Vaughn.

MRS. VAUGHN: Yes.

(*He looks at his watch. In the distance* MISS RUTH *sings "Peace Be to this Congregation."*)

DR. GREENE: Little chilly now that the sun's down. Well, I have a few more calls to make. Then I think I'll go over to the Courthouse and watch the celebration. (*He leaves.*)

MRS. VAUGHN: If you hurry you may hear Mr. Vaughn. He's making a victory speech of some kind.

(*As the lights fade,* MRS. VAUGHN *leaves.* MISS RUTH *continues to sing "Peace Be to this Congregation." From the living room* IRMA SUE *doing scales on the piano. The lights come up.*)

Scene 2

The lights come up downstage right in the living room, four months later.

ELIZABETH, *quite pregnant now, is giving a music lesson to* IRMA SUE. *Her sister,* GLADYS MAUDE, *is seated nearby, holding her music, watching.* ELIZABETH *is counting out time as* IRMA SUE *plays a piece.*

ELIZABETH: All right, girls. That will be all today. Now you both have your assignments. I won't be able to teach for a month now. I'll have to stay quiet for awhile, the doctor says, after the baby is born.

GLADYS MAUDE: When are you expecting the baby?

ELIZABETH: Anytime now.

IRMA SUE: What do you want? A boy or a girl?

ELIZABETH: Oh, I don't care.

GLADYS MAUDE: That's what Mama says. She says she never cares as long as it's healthy.

IRMA SUE: That's not what Papa says. He says he's going to blow his brains out if she has any more girls.

GLADYS MAUDE: Oh, he's just joking. You know what a joker Papa is, Miss Elizabeth.

IRMA SUE: Of course, he's joking. I know that, old ugly.

GLADYS MAUDE: Old ugly yourself. Papa is always joking or teasing about something. (*Band music is heard in the distance.*) A lot of our soldiers are home now. I bet they're glad to get back. Don't you?

ELIZABETH: I'm sure so.

GLADYS MAUDE: Did you have anyone in your family overseas?

ELIZABETH: A cousin.

GLADYS MAUDE: Was he wounded in any way?

ELIZABETH: No.

GLADYS MAUDE: My mother had a second cousin. He had a nervous breakdown in camp. Tried to shoot his best friend.

IRMA SUE: My daddy said the army wouldn't have any of his relatives. They were all in jail for stealing horses.

GLADYS MAUDE: He was only joking, of course.

IRMA SUE: Daddy says they're having too many parades now. He says people are getting tired of them. He says most of the people marching never saw France. He says those that saw France never want to see a uniform or hear a band again.

GLADYS MAUDE: Come on, Irma Sue. It's time we go now. You're talking Miss Lizzie to death.

IRMA SUE: You have a nerve criticizing anyone else for talking, the way you jabber all the time. Mama says you give her a splitting headache the way you talk all the time.

GLADYS MAUDE: I don't talk half as much as you.

IRMA SUE: You better watch out. God doesn't like liars.

GLADYS MAUDE: No, and he doesn't like Priss Ikes either. (*They start out.*)

IRMA SUE: See you in a month, Miss Lizzie.

GLADYS MAUDE: Can't wait to see your new baby.

(*They leave.* BROTHER *comes in. He is all dressed up.*)

BROTHER: Lizzie, I've come to say goodbye. I'm taking the train to Galveston in a few minutes. Papa is going to drive me down to the station. I'm sorry I won't be here when the baby comes.

ELIZABETH: You'll be back before you know it, Brother.

(*In the distance a band plays.*)

BROTHER: If I like the sea, I'm going to sign up again. Papa says it won't be long before there will be boats from

Galveston going to Europe. He says he can get me on one of them. So, I guess I'll get to see Europe after all.

(*Band music is heard again.*)

They're having another parade. Some more of the wounded soldiers came home today. Papa thinks they're running the parades into the ground. Can you ride to the station and see me off?

ELIZABETH: I think I'd better not, Brother. I don't want to get too far away from home. I wouldn't want to have my baby at the railroad station.

BROTHER (*laughing*): I guess not. (*He kisses her.*) Good-bye, Sister. Take care of yourself. Tell Horace goodbye for me.

ELIZABETH: I will. Take care of yourself now.

BROTHER: Oh, don't worry about me. I'm going to straighten out, you know. I'm going to make you all proud of me. I told Papa that last night. I said, "Papa, believe me . . ." (MR. VAUGHN *comes in.*)

MR. VAUGHN: Brother, do you know your train will be here in ten minutes? Get into the car.

BROTHER: I was just leavin', Papa. Goodbye, Elizabeth.

(*He goes out.* MR. VAUGHN *follows after him.* ELIZABETH *goes to the piano. She plays "Narcissus."* BESSIE *appears at the door.* ELIZABETH *doesn't see her, but continues playing.*)

BESSIE: Mary . . . (ELIZABETH *hears her, stops playing and turns toward her.*) You had your baby yet?

ELIZABETH: No, Bessie. Mercy, do I look like it? Don't stand out there. Come on in. (BESSIE *comes into the room and sits on a chair.*) When I have it you'll be among the first to know, Bessie. (*She laughs.*) Horace is worse than he was last time. He's a nervous wreck. "What are you so nervous about, Horace?" I ask him. "There's nothing to be afraid of. I have a very easy time. Jenny was absolutely no trouble when she was being born." But I don't think he even hears me. (*She laughs.*) And my mother. She's a better actor than Horace. She tries to pretend she's not worried, but I know she is. I can tell. She's had six children and all of them were born early and were healthy, and she had easy deliveries every time . . . (*Pause.*) Of course, two of them died later on . . . in their infancy, like Jenny. (*Pause.*) I have fears now, too, Bessie. I don't tell them that. I haven't told anyone else. I wake up in the night afraid, now. Afraid . . . (*Pause.*) I tell you now I don't want this baby if anything is going to happen to it afterwards. I don't want it at all. I couldn't stand going through again what I went through when I lost Jenny. (*Pause. She is suddenly short of breath and sits down in a chair.*) Bessie, would you go into the kitchen and get me a glass of water?

(BESSIE *goes.* ELIZABETH *seems to have a slight twinge of pain, and she hums "Narcissus" to herself.* HORACE *comes in. He has his arms filled with groceries.*)

HORACE: Hello, sweetheart. (*He kisses her. He puts the groceries on the piano.*) How does my girl feel? (BESSIE *comes in with the water.*) Hello, Bessie. I didn't know you were here. (BESSIE *gives the water to* ELIZABETH. ELIZABETH *drinks it.*)

ELIZABETH: Horace, I think you'd better run over and get Mama.

HORACE: What's wrong? Anything wrong? Should I call the doctor?

ELIZABETH: I don't think so, yet. Just get Mama for me.

(He goes running out. She drinks more of the water. HORACE *runs back in.)*

HORACE: I'm going crazy, I think. Your mother's not home. I remember I passed her in the car with your papa taking Brother to the train. Oh, my God!

ELIZABETH: Don't get excited, honey.

HORACE: Are you all right?

ELIZABETH: Yes, I'm all right.

HORACE: Why did you want your mother then?

ELIZABETH: I just felt a little something.

HORACE: Like what?

ELIZABETH: Nothing much. Just something.

HORACE: Maybe I'd better call the doctor?

ELIZABETH: Maybe you had.

(He runs out.)

BESSIE: The glass is empty. You want me to get you some more water?

ELIZABETH: No, thank you. *(Pause.)* You waited with me last time while Horace went for the doctor, remember? Only that time we weren't living in our own home, and my mother and father were out of town. *(Pause. A train whistle blows.)* There goes my brother. He's sailing for New Orleans and New York and Baltimore out of Galveston. *(Pause.)* Bessie, my fear has left me. Oh, dear God, it has left me. It's all gone. I can look on this baby now without fear. *(Pause.)* If it was a boy I had at first wanted to call it for my papa. I told Horace that, and I noticed he didn't say anything, but was kind of quiet for a week or two, I thought he was sick, and I asked him if he felt all right, and finally he told me what was wrong. He said if it was a boy he wanted it named after him. He said his mother had named him Albert after her father and he felt it had hurt his father deeply. I said you were named Horace after your father, too. (BESSIE *cries.*) Bessie . . . (BESSIE *is sobbing now.*) Why are you crying, honey?

BESSIE: I'm scared.

ELIZABETH: What of, honey?

BESSIE: I don't know. I just am.

ELIZABETH: Are you afraid because I'm going to have a baby? (*Pause.* BESSIE *continues crying.*) You weren't before. You stayed with me until the doctor arrived. Do you want to go on home, honey?

BESSIE: No Ma'am. I'm not scared of you. (*Pause.*) I passed Vernon Drayton's house today and he was in the yard and as I was passing he took a screaming fit, because his mother said he heard a noise, and he was shellshocked, and I never seen no one do that before and it scared me. (ELIZABETH *holds her in her arms.*) I don't like war if it does things like that. Do you?

ELIZABETH: No, I don't but the war's over now and they say there will never be another one.

BESSIE: I passed a colored boy uptown. I don't even know his name, but he was in uniform and he had a leg cut off and Howard Lilo lost an arm an' Jack . . .

ELIZABETH: Bessie, don't. Please, don't . . . I'm sorry, but please, please don't. I was feeling so good then, and I don't want to go back to my fears. I don't want ever . . . (*Pause.*) Do you know what will be hardest for me? Going to visit Jenny's grave afterwards. I swear to you once I do that . . . Once . . . (*Pause.*) Mrs. Merriwether told me that in five years, ten years, I'll go out there and feel nothing.

It will be just like she had never been. Mama says no. She says she never goes out there and looks at her children's graves without feeling something. It's not always the same she said. I told Horace maybe we should have a lot of children like Papa and Mama then you don't go crazy worrying about just one of them . . . but Horace says he'd go crazy if he had the responsibility for a large family like Papa does. He says he doesn't see how Papa stands it sometimes. The way his children spend money and make demands on him and . . . (*Pause.*) If it's a girl I'm going to name it after my mother. Horace was glad about that, he said. After I explained why I didn't want to name her after myself. I said since I hadn't named Jenny after myself, I felt it would be disloyal to her to ever name a child after me, and . . . (*Pause.*) I named Jenny after my little sister that died. I wish I hadn't now. I wish. (*Pause.*) It worried me so for the longest time that's why my Jenny was taken, because I named her after a dead baby . . . It bothered me so I had to go talk to the preacher and he said that was just superstition. That had nothing to do with it. That God wouldn't take a baby for something foolish like that. "Then why did God take my baby?" I asked him. He couldn't answer that. He said there was bound to be a reason, but he didn't know it. Bessie, I have to tell you this. I have to tell somebody this . . . Remember how I used to always talk to you before the other baby came? You know how happy I was about having that baby. (*Pause.*) And now, Bessie, I'm ashamed but I'm not so happy about having this baby, I don't want this baby. I want my other baby back. I want Jenny back. I don't want this baby at all. (*Pause.*) And I'm afraid of ever saying that and thinking that. Afraid that I'll be punished for not submitting to God's will in all this. That's what our minister, Mr. Myers, told us we must do . . . that I must ask God for the understanding to see His will that Jenny died. Do you believe that, Bessie? Do you believe it was

His will that Jenny died? (*Pause.*) I'll name the next baby after this one, if it's a girl, too, Corella, after Horace's mother.

(MRS. VAUGHN *comes hurrying in.*)

MRS. VAUGHN: I passed Horace running for the doctor. He told me. Don't you think you'd better lie down?

ELIZABETH: Not yet, Mama.

MRS. VAUGHN: Have your labor pains started?

ELIZABETH: Once in awhile.

MRS. VAUGHN: Then you'd better lie down. (ELIZABETH *goes upstage right to the bedroom area, and lies on the bed.* MRS. VAUGHN *sees* BESSIE.) Bessie, child. You'd better run on home now. (BESSIE *cries.*) Good Lord, what's the matter with you, Bessie? Giving birth is perfectly normal. What on earth are you crying about?

BESSIE: I don't want to go home.

MRS. VAUGHN: You have to go home. This is no place for you to be now.

BESSIE: I'm scared to go home.

MRS. VAUGHN: What in the world are you scared of?

BESSIE: Vernon. I'm scared to go past his house.

ELIZABETH: She saw him have a fit today and it frightened her.

MRS. VAUGHN: Oh, my God!

ELIZABETH: She won't be in the way. Let Horace walk her past his house when he gets here.

(HORACE *comes in.*)

HORACE: The doctor will be right here. (*He is panting and breathing heavily.*)

MRS. VAUGHN: Did you run all the way there and back?

HORACE: Every step of the way.

MRS. VAUGHN: Why didn't you use the telephone?

HORACE: That's what Dr. Greene said when I ran up to him. "Did you ever think of using the telephone?" "I was too rattled," I said, "I forgot we had a telephone." "Women have babies all over the world every minute of the day," he said. "Keep calm . . . Anyway, I've never lost a father yet," he said. (HORACE *collapses into the chair.*) How is Elizabeth?

MRS. VAUGHN: She's all right.

(DR. GREENE *comes in.*)

Hello, doctor. Elizabeth is in here.

(*They go into the bedroom.* DR. GREENE *goes over to the bed.* HORACE *stands near the door.*)

DR. GREENE: How are you, Elizabeth?

ELIZABETH: I'm all right, doctor. How are you?

DR. GREENE: I'm all right. Doctors can't afford to get sick, you know.

(BESSIE *comes to the door.*)

BESSIE: Mary . . .

ELIZABETH: Oh, Bessie, are you still here?

BESSIE: I want to go home.

HORACE: Well, go on home then, Bessie. We've got everything under control here now.

ELIZABETH: She's afraid to go home by herself, Horace.

HORACE: Why?

ELIZABETH: The Drayton boy had a fit of some kind when she went by there today and she's scared to go back alone. You take her home, Horace.

DR. GREENE: Take a good long walk while you're gone, Horace?

HORACE: Why?

DR. GREENE: Because you're too nervous. I don't want you around here just now.

HORACE: Why?

DR. GREENE: Because you get nervous and upset too easily. Now just go take a good long walk.

HORACE: How long?

DR. GREENE: An hour . . . two hours.

HORACE: An hour?

DR. GREENE: At least. (HORACE *starts out.*) And if you see Mr. Vaughn, tell him to walk with you.

HORACE (*leaving*): Come on, Bessie. We'll go the back way.

DR. GREENE: Have your labor pains started?

ELIZABETH: I think so.

DR. GREENE: Often?

ELIZABETH: Not too often.

(*Lights fade as* DR. GREENE *begins to examine* ELIZABETH.)

Scene 3

The lights come up downstage left on the graveyard plot. SAM *is there.*
HORACE *comes to graves of his family.*

SAM: I hear you're about to start your new store?

HORACE: Yes, Sam. I hope to open it in the early fall.

SAM: Don't the tombstones look nice?

HORACE: I think so.

SAM (*pointing to Jenny's grave*): That was one grave I sure
hated to dig. While I was digging it a man came over to
me and said you might as well dig one next to her for her
father. He won't last the night. Flu has him, too. Well, you
fooled them.

HORACE: Yes.

SAM: Isn't it something how it came and went. You think
the Germans sent them germs over here?

HORACE: Oh, I wouldn't think so.

(*In the distance the band plays.* MRS. BOONE *comes in. Her hair is
dyed red and pulled tight over her head. She has on a tight, flowered
dress, very high-heeled shoes, heavy rouge and lipstick. She carries a
bouquet of flowers. A ten-year-old boy, small for his age, follows shyly
behind her.*)

MRS. BOONE: Horace . . .

HORACE: Oh, hello, Mrs. Boone.

MRS. BOONE: Today was Clay's birthday. I brought some
flowers to his grave and I put some on your little girl's
grave.

HORACE: That's very kind of you, Mrs. Boone.

MRS. BOONE: Clay was the one told me she was born. I called up Mrs. Vaughn and I said I think it's time now you forgive those children, now that they have a child. You know how haughty she is. She thanked me for telling her about the baby and she said, "We have forgiven them . . . And we know all about the baby . . ." (*Pause.*) I think you and Clay were the same age.

HORACE: He was three months older.

MRS. BOONE (*turns and points to the boy*): Horace, I'm adopting this boy. His mama and daddy went off and left him, so the sheriff gave him to me to raise. My brother is raising a Mexican, but I said I wanted me a white boy.

HORACE: Hello, son. (*The boy keeps his head down and doesn't answer.*)

MRS. BOONE: Say hello to Mr. Horace, boy. He was my son's best friend. (*The boy continues holding his head down.*) Shake hands now, don't stand there with your head down like you've been caught stealing. (*The boy shyly keeps his head down and shakes hands.*) I'll have to teach him manners and everything else. I'm sure his folks was common as dirt. My shiftless brothers were very upset, of course, when they found out I had him. "Don't worry," I said, "I'm leaving everything to you and your children. Not that that will mean anything. You'll have run through it all a year after I'm dead. (*She points to the tombstones.*) You had the tombstones put on the wrong graves, Horace. Your father is in that grave and your Uncle Steve in that one and Cal in that one.

HORACE: No Ma'am. Cousin Minnie told me it was this way.

MRS. BOONE: Well, Minnie is wrong. I came to all their funerals and I remember.

MR. VAUGHN (*entering*): Horace. I've been all over town looking for you. I went to your aunt's and uncle's, to the drug store and to your shop. Someone said, "I saw him heading for the graveyard." (*He sees* MRS. BOONE.) Hello, Mrs. Boone.

MRS. BOONE: Hello, Mr. Vaughn. My porter says he saw you put Brother on the train this afternoon.

MR. VAUGHN: Yes. He went to Galveston. He takes a cotton boat from there.

HORACE: Excuse me, Mr. Vaughn. Did you want me for something?

MR. VAUGHN: What? Oh, yes, I guess I did. You're a father again, Horace.

HORACE: I am?

MR. VAUGHN: Mother and baby are doing fine. Come on. I'll drive you home.

HORACE: Yes Sir.

(*They start off. The band plays again during the rest of the scene.*)

MRS. BOONE: Mr. Vaughn . . .

MR. VAUGHN: Yes Ma'am . . .

MRS. BOONE: Was it a boy or a girl?

MR. VAUGHN: A boy.

(*They leave as the lights fade.*)

Scene 4

The lights come up upstage right in the bedroom and downstage right in the living room area. ELIZABETH *is in bed,* MRS. VAUGHN *beside her holding the baby.* DR. GREENE *is in the front room getting ready to leave. The phone rings.* MRS. VAUGHN *puts the baby beside* ELIZABETH*. She goes out to answer the phone.* HORACE *comes into the living room.*

DR. GREENE: Where did they find you?

HORACE: The cemetery.

DR. GREENE: I'm on my way. Wife and baby are doing fine.

HORACE: Thank you.

(He goes. HORACE *goes into the bedroom.* ELIZABETH *has her eyes closed, the baby beside her.* HORACE *enters. She doesn't hear him. He goes quietly over to the bed and whispers:)*

Elizabeth.

(She opens her eyes. He kisses her on the forehead. He looks at the baby beside her.)

Hello, Horace, Jr. *(To* ELIZABETH:*)* I was out at the cemetery when your daddy found me. Today was Clay's birthday. Mrs. Boone brought some flowers to his grave and then she put some on Jenny's grave. Wasn't that nice of her?

ELIZABETH: Yes.

HORACE: Mrs. Boone says Cousin Minnie was wrong and we have the tombstones on the wrong graves. Isn't that a mess?

ELIZABETH: Well, Mrs. Boone could be wrong, too.

HORACE: Of course, she could. Well, the baby wasn't born at night.

ELIZABETH: No.

HORACE: What time was he born?

ELIZABETH: At three o'clock.

HORACE: I asked Aunt Virgie when I was born and she said between four and five in the morning. She was there, she said, helping Mama. And you were born at seven in the morning?

ELIZABETH: Yes.

HORACE: Exactly at seven?

ELIZABETH: I guess so.

HORACE: I knew a boy once born on Christmas Day and another on the twenty-ninth of February. I wouldn't care to be born then. Would you?

ELIZABETH: No.

HORACE: Elizabeth . . .

ELIZABETH: Yes.

HORACE: I love you.

ELIZABETH: I love you, too.

(MR. VAUGHN *comes into the living room and into the bedroom.*)

MR. VAUGHN: Hello, Lizzie.

ELIZABETH: Hello, Papa.

MR. VAUGHN (*looking down at the baby*): He's a fine looking fellow.

MRS. VAUGHN (*entering*): Do you know who that was on the phone?

MR. VAUGHN: Who?

MRS. VAUGHN: Sister Lizzie in Houston. She said Brother had gotten off the train at Houston and had walked out to her house and didn't want to go to Galveston, said he was homesick and wanted to come home.

MR. VAUGHN: Oh, my God!

MRS. VAUGHN: So, I told her to put him on the phone and I told him to march himself down to that station and to take the next train for Galveston and not to dare show his face around here until he had gone to New York and back on that cotton boat.

MR. VAUGHN: I'm glad you did.

(*In the distance* MISS RUTH *sings "Peace Be to this Congregation."*)

ELIZABETH: Horace . . .

HORACE: Yes?

ELIZABETH: What kind of flowers did Mrs. Boone put on Jenny's grave?

HORACE: Sweet peas, cosmos, periwinkles.

(ELIZABETH *closes her eyes.*)

MRS. VAUGHN: Do you want me to take the baby so you can rest more comfortably?

ELIZABETH: No, thank you. I want to keep him next to me.

MR. VAUGHN: Looking at them like this you can't imagine anything bad happening to them, can you? No bad habits, no sickness, no killings, no wars . . .

MRS. VAUGHN: Well, everyone is saying we'll never have another war, so we won't have to worry about that for him, will we?

(*The phone rings. She goes.*)

MR. VAUGHN: They're having another parade tonight.

ELIZABETH: Are there more soldiers coming home?

MR. VAUGHN: I don't think so. They're just parading. A lot of them can't find jobs. If the poor devils could find work they wouldn't have time to parade so much.

ELIZABETH: Horace . . .

HORACE: Yes?

ELIZABETH: Sweet peas, cosmos and periwinkle . . .

HORACE: Yes, and snapdragons and verbena . . .

MRS. VAUGHN (*re-entering*): That was sister Lizzie. She says Brother left her house for Galveston.

MR. VAUGHN: Did he take the Interurban?

MRS. VAUGHN: She says he did. She says for us not to worry. She thinks he is going to turn out all right.

(MISS RUTH *is singing.*) Oh, I love that hymn Ruth is singing. (*She begins to sing with* RUTH.)

"Oh, the peace of God be near us,
Fill within our hearts Thy home.
With Thy bright appearing cheer us
In Thy blessed freedom come."

ELIZABETH (*faintly, very tired*):

"Oh, the peace of God be near us,
Fill within our hearts Thy home."
Sweet peas, cosmos, periwinkle, snapdragons,
verbena . . .

(She holds the baby close to her.)

MR. VAUGHN: Mrs. Boone is adopting a boy.

MRS. VAUGHN: I hear.

MR. VAUGHN: She had him out at the cemetery with her.

ELIZABETH *(almost asleep)*: "Oh, the peace of God be near
us . . ."

MR. VAUGHN: No more wars, no more bad habits . . .

ELIZABETH: "Fill within our hearts Thy home . . ."

*(ELIZABETH closes her eyes. She is asleep. HORACE watches his wife
and child sleeping. MR. and MRS. VAUGHN listen to MISS RUTH
as she begins the hymn again and far in the distance, the band
continues playing a patriotic song.)*